PAST IMPERFECT: FUTURE TENSE

Copyright ©1999 Spring Harvest

The authors assert the moral right to be identified as the
authors of this work.

Published by
Spring Harvest
14 Horsted Square
Uckfield
East Sussex TN22 1QL

First edition 1999

Acknowledgements
Scripture quotations taken from the HOLY BIBLE, NEW
INTERNATIONAL VERSION.
Copyright ©1973, 1978, 1984 by International Bible Society.
Used by permission of Hodder and Stoughton Limited.
All rights reserved.

"NIV" is a registered trade mark of International Bible
Society. UK trademark number 1448790

Printed and bound in Great Britain.

Spring Harvest. A Registered Charity.

ISBN   1 899788 28 X

Past Imperfect
Future Tense

Family, Church
and Society in a
New Millennium

AFTERNOON
SEMINAR
PROGRAMME

SKEGNESS 1999

Please note: not all seminars run all weeks.
See your Programme Planner for details.

SPRING HARVEST

Equipping the Church for action

PRESSURE POINTS

Seminars designed to let God change us and heal us for the new millennium

PRESSURE IN MY RELATIONSHIPS...

1 Making marriage work in a stressed-out age.

2 Coping with divorce in a stressed-out age.

3 Being a decent parent in a stressed-out age.

FURTHER READING

Rob Parsons, *The sixty minute marriage* (Hodder); Robert Warren, *Divorce and Remarriage : policy options* (Grove); Andrew Cornes, *Questions about Divorce and Re-marriage* (Monarch); Alan Storkey, *The Meanings of Love* (IVP)

PRESSURE IN MY PERSONAL LIFE...

1 What does it mean to be a man in a stressed-out age?

2 What does it mean to be a woman in a stressed-out age?

FURTHER READING

Roy McCloughry, *Men and Masculinity* (Hodder); Rosie Nixson, *Liberating the gospel for women* (Grove); Ann Brown, *Apology to women* (IVP); Anne Borrowdale, *Distorted Images* (SPCK); Jennifer Beresford, *Creating confidence in women* (SPCK); Roy Mc Cloughry, *Man and Masculinity* (o/p); Peter Meadows, *Pressure Points* (Word); Polly Ghazi and Judy Jones, *Downshifting - the guide to simpler happier living* (Coronet)

PRESSURE IN MY CIRCUMSTANCES...

1 Managing money in a stressed-out age.

2 Dealing with disappointment in a stressed-out age.

FURTHER READING

Keith Tondeur, *Escape from debt* (EA); John Houghton, *Handling your money* (Word UK); Philip Yancey, *Where is God when it hurts?* (Marshall Pickering); Russ Parker, *Free to Fail* (Triangle); Keith Tondeur, *Your Money and Your Life* (Triangle)

PRESSURE IN MY RELATIONSHIP WITH GOD...

1 Is God there? – dealing with doubt.

2 Is God real? – when prayer and worship stop making sense.

3 Is God evil? – making sense of suffering.

FURTHER READING

Jenny Francis, *Belief beyond pain* (Triangle); Peter Cottrell, *Is God helpless?* (Triangle); Jennifer Rees Larcombe, *Where have you gone, God?* (Hodder); Gordon MacDonald, *Restoring Your Spiritual Passion* (Highland)

PRESSURE IN MY HOME...

1 Divided families

FURTHER READING

Myra Chave-Jones, *Living with anger* (Triangle)

PRESSURE FROM WITHIN...

1 Drugs and addiction

FURTHER READING

Peter Meadows, *Pressure Points* (Word UK); Marion Ashton, *A Mind at Ease* (Over Comer Pubs)

R. OTHER SEMINARS

1 Millennium: Millennium Clinic.

Copyright ©1999 Spring Harvest

Spring Harvest
14 Horsted Square
Uckfield
East Sussex TN22 1QL
Spring Harvest. A Registered Charity.

Equipping the Church for action

PAST IMPERFECT:

FUTURE TENSE

FAMILY, CHURCH AND SOCIETY IN A NEW MILLENNIUM

compiled and edited by
Stephen Gaukroger and Peter Meadows

CONTRIBUTORS

Dr Michael Moynagh   Canon Dr Christina Baxter
Dr Christine Sine   Rev Dr Derek Tidball
Dr Tom Sine   Alan Storkey

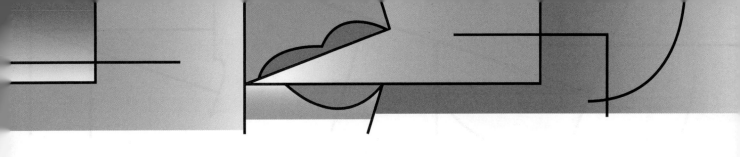

CONTENTS

INTRODUCTION

INTRODUCTION

ONE THING IS CERTAIN ABOUT THE FUTURE. IT WILL NOT BE SIMPLY MORE OF THE PRESENT

A very different world is charging towards us. The change is going to be more than cosmetic – with things done differently as a matter of taste. The changes will be fundamental, like arriving in a strange new world.

In a way we never have experienced before:–

The planet is being wired into a single global electronic nervous system. Satellite, the internet and micro optics are knitting us into one single global electronic order.

On the way is a new global economy. With the end of the cold war virtually all nations, including those of the UK, suddenly joined the free market race to the top, becoming part of a new global economic order. A butterfly flaps its wings in Tokyo and redundancies break out in Swindon.

The gulf between the richest and the poorest nations widens. And the West can afford to send less aid.

An increasingly lost world is ahead. Global population growth is outstripping the Church's best efforts to

---

FACTS

Ten Global Terms for 2020

Superclass:	a global elite with very high incomes
Friction-free Capitalism:	commerce made easier and cheaper by the internet
Knowbots:	intelligent computers filtering out unwanted emails
Walton Family Household:	multi-generational homes
Gated Communities:	secure housing projects giving protection from crime
Lifestyle Communities:	housing based on shared interests, such as golf villages
Misery Gap:	the difference between pensions and the money needed for a comfortable retirement
Contingent Workforce:	the majority of workers on short-term contracts
Cyber Schools:	home or classroom-based online lessons
Personal Privatisation:	increased responsibility for pensions, health and education costs.

From *The Times Online*, David Charter, Education Correspondent. 26 April 1998.

reach the whole world with the gospel. While more than a quarter of our global population identify themselves as Christian, population growth defies our efforts to reach them with the Christian message.

Our UK society is turning upside down. A growing range of societal issues are set to impact the UK. These include increasing job insecurity, persistent unemployment and a breakdown in stable family relationships.

SHOULD WE BOTHER ABOUT THE FUTURE?

Some people see it as pointless to think about the future. Isn't it all out of our control, anyway? It can also seem a little frightening. So why bother?

There are good reasons for thinking about the future, especially as Christians:

Thinking about the future helps you to understand the present.

Imagining what the present might become helps you notice significant developments that need responding to in the here and now. For example,

> BT Laboratories predict that people born in 2015 will live for 100 years. So who will be able to afford to retire at 60 when they have another 40 years to live? And what must be done now for people to cope when it happens?

Thinking about the future helps you to shape what is ahead.

On current trends, the growth in car ownership will make traffic congestion in parts of Britain almost unbearable by 2020. So what can we do now, as a society, to make sure this does not happen?

Thinking about the future puts us on God's agenda.

It is God's future – he wants to save it and make it holy. And he wants us to help shape it and celebrate in it for his purposes.

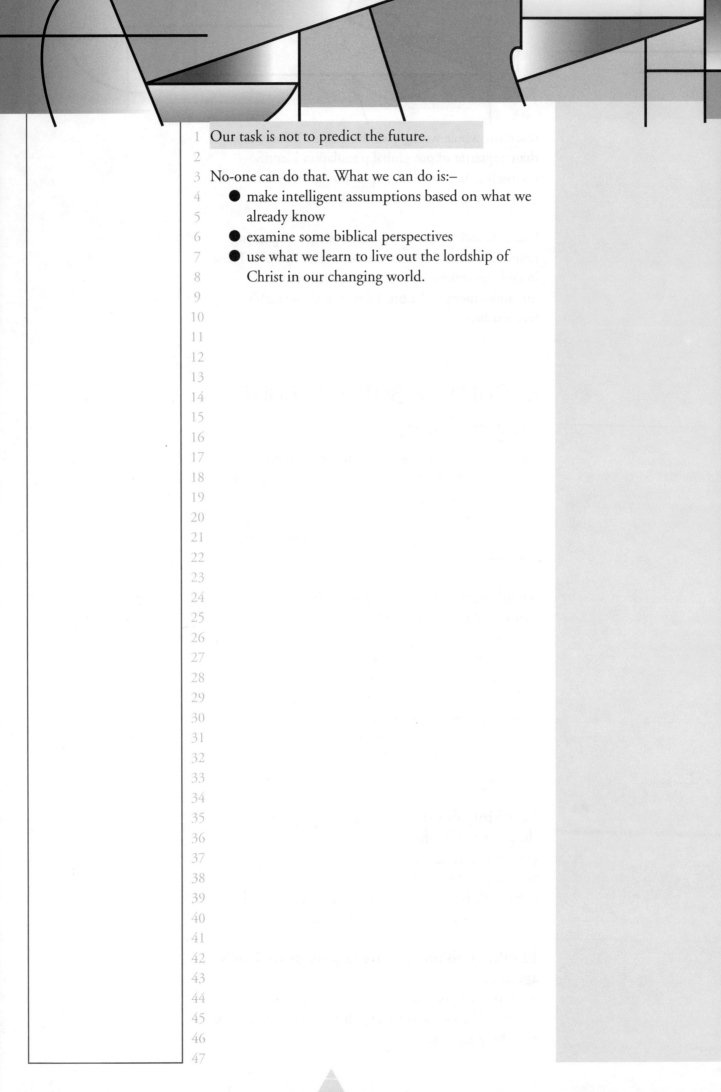

1   Our task is not to predict the future.

2

3   No-one can do that. What we can do is:–

4   ● make intelligent assumptions based on what we

5   already know

6   ● examine some biblical perspectives

7   ● use what we learn to live out the lordship of

8   Christ in our changing world.

9

10

11

12

13

14

15

16

17

18

19

20

21

22

23

24

25

26

27

28

29

30

31

32

33

34

35

36

37

38

39

40

41

42

43

44

45

46

47

THE CHURCH

QUESTION ?

Is this the future of the Church? And how do we feel about it? Is it a future which will go away if we ignore it, or are there alternatives? And who cares?

Email from Steve Hayes to Adrian Chatfield, 4 May 1998.

THE FUTURE OF THE CHURCH

THE PARISH CHURCH OF ST INTERNET?

Two generations ago, the American concept of drive-in movies led to drive-in churches there.

The internet is the new medium impacting the Church.

- One out of six American teenagers expect to use the internet as a substitute for their current church-based activities within the next five years, according to a recent survey.
- More than one in ten American adults already use the internet for religious purposes, mainly to discuss religious ideas and experiences with others.

George Barna, president of the company conducting the surveys, comments; "… by 2010 we will probably have 10 per cent to 20 per cent of the population relying primarily or exclusively on the internet for its religious input. Those people will never set foot on a church campus."

The UK picture
In the West, organised religion is in decline. And where does the UK fit in the picture?

FACTS

Table 1:
UK Religious Community 1975–2000 (millions)

	1975		1985		1995		2000[1]	
Christian (Trinitarian)	40.2	72%	39.1	69%	38.1	65%	37.8	64%
Non-Trinitarian[2]	0.7	1%	1.0	2%	1.3	2%	1.4	2%
Non-Christian religions	1.4	3%	2.2	3%	2.8	5%	3.1	5%
Hindu	0.3		0.4		0.4		0.5	
Jew	0.4		0.3		0.3		0.3	
Muslim	0.4		0.9		1.2		1.4	
Sikh	0.2		0.3		0.6		0.6	
Others	0.1		0.3		0.3		0.3	
Total all religions	42.3	76%	42.3	74%	42.2	72%	42.2	71%

Source: UK Christian Handbook 1998/99, p.12

(1)   Estimate.
(2)   Non-Trinitarian are those groups who draw on the Christian tradition but do not subscribe to the traditional Christian belief in one God who is three persons, Father, Son and Holy Spirit. Britain is still largely a "Christian" country, as the chart shows.

Despite all the new churches being planted, about one a week at present, and the exciting stories of churches which are growing, overall Christianity is in retreat.

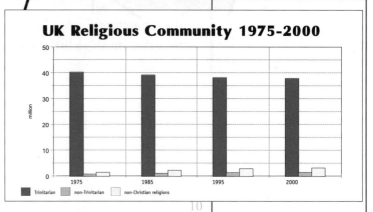

Table 1

While many cities feel distinctly multi-faith, about two-thirds of the population still see themselves as being part of the Christian community. However:–

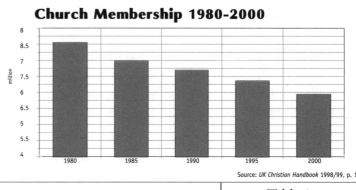

Source: *UK Christian Handbook* 1998/99, p. 13.

Table 2

- For every hundred people who regarded themselves as Christian in 1975, only 93 did in 1995.
- Table 2 shows, in terms of church membership, total membership is expected to drop from around 7.5 million in 1980 to about 5.9 million in 2000. In other words, for every 100 church members in 1980, there will only be 79 in 2000.
- In terms of the number of adults attending church, this will have fallen from 4.8 million in 1980 (11% of the population) to 3.8 million in 2000 (8%) – a decline of a fifth. This fall may partly be because of a move towards church-goers attending once or twice a month, instead of weekly as in the past.

Peter Brierley, "Please postpone the wake", *Church Times*, 14 November 1997, pp. 14-15.

Table 3

For those who express their links with the Church by having their baby baptised, usually in the Church of England, the decline is stunning. As Table 3 shows, over the last 50 years the proportion of the population baptized in

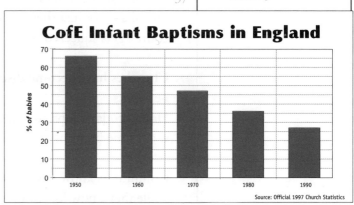

Source: Official 1997 Church Statistics

the Church of England as babies has dropped from
over two-thirds to little more than a quarter.

WHY IS THE CHURCH IN DECLINE?
A decline like this does not just 'happen'.

There is a growing suspicion of authority
The media exposes us to a vast range of conflicting
ideas and "expert" opinions. How can we know who is
right and whom to trust? And why trust an
organisation that claims to be the only one who is
right?

Choice has become a key value
Since the war, consumerism has widened choice
incredibly. Everyone now has the right to choose. This
encourages a "self-spirituality" in which people
construct their own pot-pourri of beliefs. Religion is a
matter of choosing "what works for me", not being
told what to believe.

Churches face intensive competition
There is now so much more for people to do in their
spare time. They can watch TV, hire a video, go to the
cinema, have a curry, shop till they drop, go away
more often at weekends and so on. And the
universality of the motor car adds to the array of
options.

Work and leisure patterns have changed
Shift work, rolling rotas, Sunday shopping and sport
all affect the likelihood of people attending church.
Large numbers of women now work to sustain this
lifestyle. For many people life seems frantically busy as
they juggle work, family and a plethora of leisure
pursuits – not just their own, but their children's. The
church gets squeezed out.

**Churches have become disconnected from the new
networks**
Half of today's jobs are taken by women, who once
spent time building up the local community.

Commuters know fewer people where they live. So
while they know lots of people – at work, the Church

is nowhere to be seen.

The Church has become an institution
The Church has become more of a club for those who are religious, rather than a dynamic, life-enhancing, faith-sharing company of committed friends.

A greying Church
Not only is the Church losing members, those who remain are older than the population in general. In particular, the under 35s are desperately under-represented. If the Church in the UK is to have a future, it will take a dramatic increase of investment in resources, church planting, evangelism and the development of younger leadership.

ARE CHURCHES DOOMED?
Some are pessimistic about the Church's future. They think spiritual values have been sidelined by our crass materialistic culture.

Yet there is plenty of evidence that many people have a deep spiritual hunger.

An extensive survey in 1990 found that:–
- Seven out of ten reported a belief in God;
- Over half defined themselves as religious;
- Over half regularly felt the need for prayer, meditation or contemplation;
- Over one in three often thought about the meaning and purpose of life.

Grace Davie, *Religion in Britain since 1945*, Blackwell, 1994, p. 78.

The challenge is for Christians to connect with these spiritual instincts.

Some fear that consumer values are so deeply entrenched that evangelism will never make much headway.

These values are sometimes referred to as "postmodern" and represent a hostile environment for the Church and its message. They include the beliefs that:–

> **Truth is subjective.**
> There are no objective truths "out there" which

1
2
3
4
5
6
7
8
9
10
11
12
13
14
15
16
17
18
19
20
21
22
23
24
25
26
27
28
29
30
31
32
33
34
35
36
37
38
39
40
41
42
43
44
45
46
47

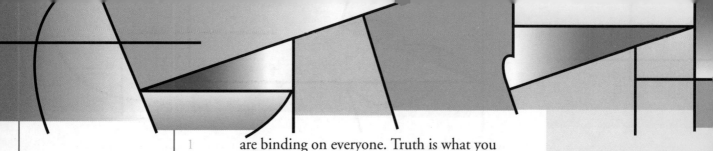

are binding on everyone. Truth is what you think it is. Just as there is no right and wrong brand of soup, there is no right and wrong about truth.

Pleasure counts.
We are moving away from a culture where there was a strong sense of moral obligation – "I ought to do such and such". In its place is one where almost everything we buy is designed to give pleasure to our senses. Pleasure guides our behaviour, rather than the moral duty which Christians have emphasised.

Appearance is all.
Our consumer culture prizes things that are packaged well, and is impressed by people who are well turned out. The Church constantly falls short of public expectations in this area. And even offers discipleship that aims to form Christian character rather than credibility.

The individual rules.
Consumer choice puts the emphasis on the "me" who chooses. "I can decide what I want". That reduces our commitment to other people. "If the church no longer suits me, I can choose to leave" rather than, "I am committed to this group and will work things through with them through thick and thin".

However, the world of work depends on values that point in the opposite direction to what society prizes.

At work:
There *are* absolute truths.
Success is a Good Thing, the "bottom line", the laws of the market, for instance. Truth is not just personal opinion.

Morality *is* important.
There are codes of conduct, professional ethics, grievance procedures, equal opportunities policies, questions about sexual harassment and so on. Successful firms have the ethic of consumer service at their core. The consumer says "I want," to which the workplace responds,

"We serve".

Reputation depends on what lies *behind* appearances.
Quality control is a top issue, for example, for much of the food industry. It's no good packaging the meat to look good if your customers get food poisoning when they eat it!

FACTS

Workplace and consumer values

Workplace values	Consumer values
Truth is objective	Truth is subjective
Morality matters	Pleasure counts
Substance counts more than appearance	Appearance is all
Team-work is vital	The individual rules

The individual *cannot* rule.
Increasingly, the success of organisations depends on the effectiveness of their teams. Research shows that the importance of interpersonal skills at work grew markedly between 1992 and 1997 (see Page 21). The individual has to fit in with other people.

Francis Green et al, "Are British Workers Getting More Skilled?" in A.B.Atkinson & John Hills (eds), *Exclusion, Employment and Opportunity*, LSE, 1998, p. 118.

This suggests that people would connect more easily with the gospel if it were presented to them in a workplace context.

Could there be hope?
There are encouraging signs that the Church is starting to meet people on their own ground.
- Some congregations worship in pubs.
- Others are discussing with local supermarkets whether Christians can organise weekend creches for busy shoppers.
- Others are beginning to reach into the workplace, for example, by encouraging older Christians to mentor younger ones.
- The Alpha course – and similar initiatives – are helping thousands to find faith.
- Increasingly, churches are making new initiatives to be open and relevant to those prepared to ask questions about faith and belief.

HOW COULD IT TURN OUT?

Here are two possible ways the Church might look in 2020.

Scenario 1 – Consumer Church

More churches will take seriously the way people are into entertainment, seeing this both as a vehicle for reaching people and a partial expression of God's character.

God wants us to enjoy ourselves. So church will be made both biblical and pleasurable.

Soon after 2010, huge flat TV screens will become available at affordable prices, and gradually replace the OHP. As a result:–

- Worship becomes more visual.
- Bible readings are animated, so that you can see the story as well as hear it.
- Difficult Bible passages are illustrated visually.
- Alongside Music Directors, some of the larger churches appoint Visual Directors, whose task is to help ministers and others make worship more visually attractive. They download interesting material from the internet.
- Sermons include video clips taken from the internet or rented videos.
- Some preachers put their material on the internet for other churches to use.
- Newcomers to church find sermons more interesting and easier to understand.

Church planting in the 1980s and '90s often created congregations for particular groups of people – a specific housing estate or families who attended a particular school, for example. By 2020 churches will be more explicit about the particular groups in the locality they want to reach. As a result:–

- Youth congregations for the over 16s are widespread. As are congregations for the younger teens.
- Special congregations exist even for 7- to 11-year-olds – who have their own sub-culture.

There will be howls of anguish from adults who resent the fragmentation of the "church family". But others

say that if you want to reach a fragmented society you
must accept a fragmented church.

Local churches become more effective at reaching
people in the midst of the consumer culture.
Successful churches are the ones that respond to unmet
needs in the consumer culture.

- They run creches, Sunday clubs and other
  children's activities for shoppers – establishing
  links with parents who are invited to church
  events.
- They are involved with after-school clubs for
  children doing home-work – providing a means
  of reaching young people.
- They establish hospitality groups for newcomers
  to the town or city who want to make friends,
  but find it difficult to meet people.

In some ways, this scenario develops the more
innovative practices of churches today. It partly
depends, however, on local churches being willing to
work together, since some of the ideas would be
difficult for a church to do on its own.

Scenario 2 – The Workplace Church
This scenario takes people by surprise. It involves
churches whose main activities are on a weekday.

More and more people join
churches which meet during the
week. These are not churches
which have their main services
on Sunday, supplemented by a
series of midweek activities.

- Some meet for an hour
  first thing on Monday,
  before people scatter –
  sometimes round the
  world – for the rest of the
  week.
- Others meet straight after
  work on a Tuesday or
  Wednesday.
- A few meet in the lunch
  hour, though that is
  generally not long enough.

FACTS

A successful Alpha course in a city
centre decided to go on meeting on
Wednesday evenings. The church
leadership turned it into an
experimental, midweek church plant
to help those who found it difficult
to attend church on Sunday. The
results surprised everyone.
Then they got stuck into workplace
issues. The Christians really enjoyed
it and began to experience the
power of God literally at work. And
non-believers were drawn into the
faith.
The church grew rapidly, others
across the UK took note and the
rest, as they say, is history.

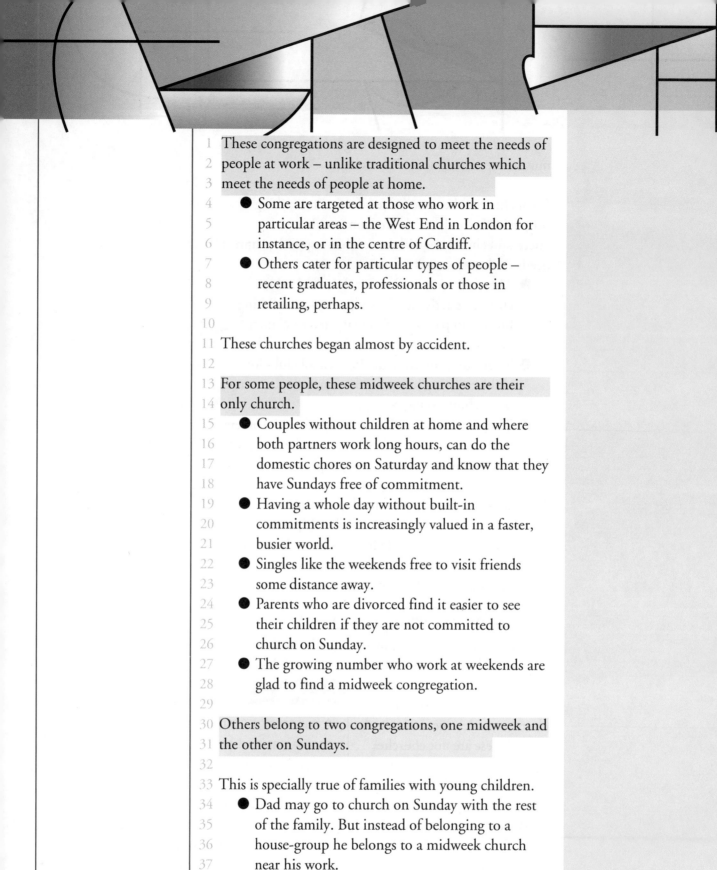

1 These congregations are designed to meet the needs of
2 people at work – unlike traditional churches which
3 meet the needs of people at home.

4 ● Some are targeted at those who work in
5 particular areas – the West End in London for
6 instance, or in the centre of Cardiff.

7 ● Others cater for particular types of people –
8 recent graduates, professionals or those in
9 retailing, perhaps.

11 These churches began almost by accident.

13 For some people, these midweek churches are their
14 only church.

15 ● Couples without children at home and where
16 both partners work long hours, can do the
17 domestic chores on Saturday and know that they
18 have Sundays free of commitment.

19 ● Having a whole day without built-in
20 commitments is increasingly valued in a faster,
21 busier world.

22 ● Singles like the weekends free to visit friends
23 some distance away.

24 ● Parents who are divorced find it easier to see
25 their children if they are not committed to
26 church on Sunday.

27 ● The growing number who work at weekends are
28 glad to find a midweek congregation.

30 Others belong to two congregations, one midweek and
31 the other on Sundays.

33 This is specially true of families with young children.

34 ● Dad may go to church on Sunday with the rest
35 of the family. But instead of belonging to a
36 house-group he belongs to a midweek church
37 near his work.

38 ● Sunday churches focus more on children and
39 older people – the spread of teenage and
40 children's congregations is one result of this.
41 While the needs of working adults are
42 increasingly met by midweek congregations.

44 Their services are highly visual, as in the previous
45 "consumer church" scenario.

47 Because they meet in hired rooms or halls, rather than

traditional church buildings, the flat screens – the size of a huge picture – feel less out of place.

The congregations are smaller than many conventional churches – perhaps between 30 and 50 people. This means they are not always blessed with gifted musicians. However, worship videos can be shown on the flat screen – so the congregation feels led by top Christian musicians.

Many churches are led by part-time or spare-time ministers, overseen and supported by full-time clergy if they belong to a denomination.

Worshippers keep in touch with each other by e-mail through the week.
- Prayer triplets exchange e-mail prayers, and internet-based home groups spring up.
- Those who are away on business still have fellowship with others, even though they cannot meet face-to-face.
- Instead of having to block out a time to meet in a hectic schedule, people can snatch moments to "hear" other people's prayers or contributions to the discussion — and make their own input.
- Those too shy to have their voice heard in a small group now contribute on equal terms.

These churches are more effective evangelistically than traditional ones.

They lay on training sessions to address people's needs at work. These include:–
- Seminars on beating stress, on managing your boss, on improving your networking skills, on how set up your own business, on being a good team– member and many others.
- A course with implicit Christian values. With an extra session at the end for those wanting to discover spiritual resources to help them put into practice what they have learnt.

Christians find it very easy to invite their work colleagues to these events, for which employers often give time off because they count as training. For many, they become stepping stones to faith. Hardly anyone says, "I don't know who to invite".

1 These churches are controversial, however.
2   ● They are accused of fragmenting the Christian
3   family.
4   ● It is said the Biblical model is for people of
5   different ages and different backgrounds to meet
6   together.
7   ● Others say that churches have always been
8   fragmented between different congregations,
9   that Christians are called to take Christ into the
10   fragments of society and that, once in the
11   fragments, the challenge is to try and draw the
12   fragments together. But you can't do that unless
13   you are in the fragments first.
14 In 2020 the Evangelical Alliance launches an initiative
15 to draw the two sides of the debate together.
16

Reactions?

18 These scenarios are not predictions of what will
19 happen. They simply illustrate what **could** happen. Are
20 they plausible? And what issues do they raise for
21 churches to think about today?

24

GOD'S GOOD INTENTIONS FOR THE CHURCH

THE CHURCH AND THE HEART OF GOD

A people for himself

The origins of the Church lie in the eternal heart of God.

- He created people in his own image so he could relate to them (Gen 1:26–28).
- When the human race's relationship with him was disrupted by sin (Gen 3:1–24), God chose Abraham's family to be his people in a special way – to receive his blessing and be a blessing to others (Gen 12:1–3).

They were:–

- his covenant people (Exod 19:5–6).
- chosen by grace (Deut 7:7).
- those who accepted the covenant obligations of loving and obeying him exclusively (Deut 29; Neh 8).

A holy people, a nation of priests

Israel, the collective name given to Abraham's descendants, were chosen not so they could enjoy special privileges but to perform a special role.

They were:–

- to be holy (Exod 19:6; Lev 19:1,20:7–8).
- to be 'set apart' for God. That's what holiness means.
- to adopt a lifestyle radically different from that of the surrounding nations (Lev 18:1–5).
- to be priests (Exod 19:6) whose community life centred on worshipping God (Exod 7:16). That's why the tabernacle was at the centre of their camp and the temple at the centre of their

1
2
3
4
5
6
7
8
9
10
11
12
13
14
15
16
17
18
19
20
21
22
23
24
25
26
27
28
29
30
31
32
33
34
35
36
37
38
39
40
41
42
43
44
45
46
47

Genesis 1:26–28
Then God said, "Let us make man in our image, in our likeness, and let them rule over the fish of the sea and the birds of the air, over the livestock, over all the earth, and over all the creatures that move along the ground." So God created man in his own image, in the image of God he created him; male and female he created them. God blessed them and said to them, "be fruitful and increase in number; fill the earth and subdue it. Rule over the fish of the sea and the birds of the air and over every living creature that moves on the ground."

Exodus 19:5–6
"'Now if you obey me fully and keep my covenant, then out of all nations you will be my treasured possession. Although the whole earth is mine, you will be for me a kingdom of priests and a holy nation.' These are the words you are to speak to the Israelites."

Leviticus 19:1
The LORD said to Moses, "Speak to the entire assembly of Israel and say to them: 'Be holy because I, the LORD your God, am holy.'"

Exodus 19:6
"'You will be for me a kingdom of priests and a holy nation.' These are the words you are to speak to the Israelites."

Exodus 7:16
"Then say to him, 'The LORD, the God of the Hebrews, has sent me to say to you: Let my people go, so that they may worship me in the desert. But until now you have not listened.'"

1 national life.
2 ● as priests, to stand between God and the world,
3   interceding for the world before God and
4   teaching the world about God.
5

The New Covenant

7 The failure of Israel to live up to her calling led God to
8 bring into being a new covenant – a two-way binding
9 agreement (Jer 31:31–34). So far as this covenant was
10 concerned:–
11 ● It was no longer tied to Israel as a nation
12   (Rom 9:6).
13 ● Gentiles as well as Jews could be members on an
14   equal footing (Gal 3:28; Eph 2:11–22).
15 ● It was brought into being by God's grace
16   (Eph 1:3–14; 2:1–10).
17 ● It was signed by the blood of Jesus
18   (1 Cor 11:25).
19 ● It was a covenant much more marvellous than
20   the old one, as Hebrews and 2 Cor 3:4–18
21   explain in great detail.
22
23 This international community of grace was composed
24 of people who:–
25 ● acknowledge Jesus as Lord (1 Cor 3:16).
26 ● have the Holy Spirit living in them (1 Cor 3:16).
27 ● are the new holy nation and royal priesthood
28   (1 Pet 2:9).
29

Loved from Eternity

31 Paul's letter to the Christians in Ephesus sets out the
32 New Testament's fullest understanding of the church.
33 It shows the Church:–
34 ● to be chosen from eternity, not an afterthought
35   (1:4–14; 3:11).
36 ● to possess a glorious heritage and experience a
37   mighty power (1:15–23).
38 ● to be God's handiwork (2:10).
39 ● to cross over racial, social and cultural barriers
40   (2:11–21).
41 ● to have a cosmic role (3:10).
42 ● to need to work at unity (4:1–6).
43 ● to possess spiritual gifts (4:11–13).
44 ● to live a distinctive lifestyle, of holiness and love
45   (4:17–5:1).
46 ● to be lights to the world (5:8–20).
47 ● to engage in spiritual warfare (6:10–18).

Jeremiah 31:31–34
"The time is coming," declares the LORD, "when I will make a new covenant with the house of Israel and with the house of Judah. It will not be like the covenant I made with their forefathers when I took them by the hand to lead them out of Egypt, because they broke my covenant, though I was a husband to them," declares the LORD. "This is the covenant that I will make with the house of Israel after that time," declares the LORD. "I will put my law in their minds and write it on their hearts. I will be their God, and they will be my people. No longer will a man teach his neighbour, or a man his brother, saying, 'Know the LORD,' because they will all know me, from the least of them to the greatest," declares the LORD. "For I will forgive their wickedness and will remember their sins no more."

1 Corinthians 3:16
Don't you know that you yourselves are God's temple and that God's Spirit lives in you?

1 Peter 2:9
But you are the chosen people, a royal priesthood, a holy nation, a people belonging to God, that you may declare the praises of him who called you out of darkness into his wonderful light.

Ephesians 2:10
For we are God's workmanship. created in Christ Jesus to do good works, which God prepared in advance for us to do.

Ephesians 3:10
His intent was that now, through the church, the manifold wisdom of God should be made known to the rulers and authorities in the heavenly realms.

26

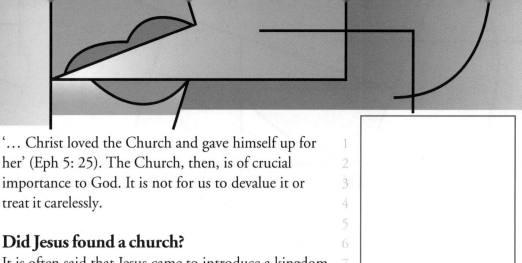

'… Christ loved the Church and gave himself up for her' (Eph 5: 25). The Church, then, is of crucial importance to God. It is not for us to devalue it or treat it carelessly.

Did Jesus found a church?

It is often said that Jesus came to introduce a kingdom not to establish a church. He seems to say little about the Church. But that's a superficial understanding.

The Church and the kingdom

The kingdom is the sphere in which God reigns and that assumes a community of people who actively place themselves under his rule.

The kingdom is not an abstract idea but one which finds a variety of tangible expressions in the world.

The Church, then, is:–
- the showcase of the kingdom, displaying to the world what God's reign is like.
- the agent of the kingdom, extending God's reign in the world.

Jesus and community

Jesus did not call isolated individuals but chose twelve disciples (Mark 3: 13–19) and had other followers who were committed to him and one another (Luke 8: 1–3; 10: 1–25). Jesus used community language in speaking about them. His disciples were:–
- Family (Mark 10:29–31).
- Brotherhood and sisterhood (Matt 23:8).
- Flock (Luke 12:32; John 10:1–21).
- City (Matt 5:14).
- Branches of a vine (John 15:5).
- Close and intimate friends (John 15:15–16).

The Sermon on the Mount (Matt 5–7) sets out the lifestyle of those who belong to the community of Jesus.

Jesus and the Church

According to Matthew's Gospel, Jesus twice refers directly to the Church in his teaching. In Matt 16:18, he says the Church is founded on the confession made by Peter – that Jesus is the Christ. He stresses the power of the Church to survive and triumph against

27

all natural and supernatural powers. In Matt 18:15, Jesus sets out guidelines about handling conflict in the church. And makes clear that the Church should strive to be a community which always aims at reconciliation.

The Birth of the Church

With the coming of the Holy Spirit at the Feast of Pentecost, a new movement is born and a new community – the Church – comes into being.

This was not an organisation or a programme of activities. It was a fabric of relationships in which fellow learners lived out their lives together.

From the very beginning, there are clear signs that this new messianic community of Jesus is going to be an international movement bursting the wineskins of traditional Judaism… . This community is radically different from the world around it; it is a living foretaste of the promised future of God.

What Paul says about the Church

A community of grace

The Church is the community of men and women called into fellowship – a costly sharing partnership – with Jesus Christ (1 Cor 1:9).

What qualifies people for such a relationship is not their own achievements, but his grace (1 Cor 1: 3; Eph 2: 8–9; Phil 1: 7; Col 1: 6). Consequently:

- The Church can never be a place of judgemental attitudes, personal superiority and rules and regulations.
- The Church is called to mirror in its relationship with other people the experience of forgiveness and undeserved favour she herself has experienced through Christ.

Ekklesia

A common Greek word for church is *ekklesia*. It means 'a community that is called out.' Paul uses the word *ekklesia* 62 out of the 114 times it is used in the New Testament. It refers to the actual meeting of the Church as a local congregation (Rom 16:5; 1 Cor 1:2; 1 Thess 1:1,2; 2 Thess 2:1; Phm 2). This shows us that the Church is not an abstract 'invisible' body but a

Live It Up! How to Create a Life You Can Love, Tom Sine, Herald Press 1994

1 Corinthians 1:9
God, who has called you into fellowship with his Son Jesus Christ our Lord, is faithful.

group of real human beings who relate to one another.

Dimensions of the Church

When Paul wants to talk about more than one church. He normally talks about the churches or congregations (plural) in Galatia or wherever (1 Cor 16:1,19; Gal 1:2; 2 Thess 2:14).

While Paul's major focus is on the local congregation, that is not the whole story.

A full picture leads us to see the Church as:–
- local (see above).
- global (1 Cor 10:32, 15:9; Gal 1:13).
- cosmic/heavenly (Eph 1:22, 2:6, 3:10; Col 1:18, 3:1–2).

From Rom 16:4,16; Gal 1:22; 1 Thess 2:14 it seems various churches have formed special associations, either with distinct characteristics or for particular purposes. Perhaps denominations are not quite so foreign to the New Testament as we have imagined.

Pictures of the Church

Much of Paul's teaching about the Church takes the form of picture language. He does not present us with a systematic statement but a kaleidoscope of images.

The Church is not an organisation with a tight constitution, set of bylaws and defined inflexible structure. It is a living community.

To Paul, the Church is best understood as:–
- a temple (1 Cor 3:16–17; 2 Cor 6:16–18; Eph 2:21).
- a new race/humanity (Rom 5:12–17; Eph 2:15).
- a body (Rom 12:4–5; 1 Cor 12:12–31; Col 1:18).
- a household (1 Tim 3:15).
- a bride (2 Cor 11:2).
- a field (1 Cor 3:9).
- an army (Gal 5:25–6:5; Eph 6:10–18).

Paul's great concern

When reading Paul's letters you learn little about the way the Church should be organised. Rather, his dominant concern is for the quality of relationships within the church.

Although composed of forgiven and converted people (1 Cor 6:11), the Church's members remain far from perfect. They struggle with:–

- the traces of their past pre-Christian way of living.
- the new demands of forming a community with others who may be very different from them but share a common commitment to Jesus. Key passages are Gal 3:13–15; Eph 4:1–4; Phil 4:2–4 and Col 3:12–16.

Hence, much of Paul's teaching concentrates on:–

- Humility.
- Gentleness.
- Patience.
- Forgiveness.
- Integrity.
- Service.
- Bearing one another's burdens.
- Love.

Similarly, Paul gives instructions on how people in various social relationships and positions in life should behave. The gospel has clearly changed those relationships. Key passages are Eph 5:21–6:9; Col 3:18–4:1; 1 Tim 5:1–6:2; Tit 2:1–10 and Philemon.

HOW THE CHURCH OPERATED

We know little of the actual life of the Early Church. But some important things can be discovered in the New Testament.

Acts 2:42 tells us their primary concerns, as they met together, were:–

- The apostles' teaching.
- Fellowship.
- Breaking of bread.
- Prayer.

That is certainly reflected elsewhere. We know they:–

- engaged in worship in which many participated (1 Cor 14:13–33; Eph 5:19; Col 3:16).
- celebrated agapé meals and the Lord's Supper (1

QUESTION ?

What about groups of churches functioning together, in the way we think of denominations or "streams"?

Acts 2:42
They devotes themselves to the apostles' teaching and to the fellowship, to the breaking of bread and to prayer.

Cor 11:17–34).

- practised baptism (Acts 8:36–39; Rom 6:1–4; 1 Cor 1:12:1–14:39).
- exercised the gifts of the Spirit (1 Cor 12:1–14:40).
- met on Sundays, the day of resurrection (Acts 20:7; 1 Cor 16:2).
- collected for fellow Christians in need (1 Cor 16:1–2; 2 Cor 8–9).
- listened to the reading of Scripture (Col 4:16; 1 Thess 5:27; 1 Tim 4:13; 2 Pet 3:16).
- heard the message of Jesus expounded (Acts 20:7; 1 Cor 1:13–17; 1 Tim 4:11–14; 2 Tim 2:14–19).
- admonished and exhorted one another (Col 3;16; Rom 15:14; 1 Cor 4:31; 1 Thess; 4:18; 5:11,14).
- prayed for those in authority as well as in the Church (1 Cor 11:5; 14:13–15; 2 Tim 2:1–4).
- exercised discipline over members (Acts 5:1–11; 1 Cor 5:1–13).

The Early Church had no buildings of their own.

They met in the houses of its wealthier members such as Stephanus or Nympha (Rom 16:3–5,14,15; 1 Cor 16:19; Col 4:15; Phm 2).

Early Christian congregations may have been quite small and composed of people who naturally belonged to one of the multitude of social networks in a city. The household was a key social institution in the day and a natural social unit to use as the basis for mission and the formation of the Church.

Use of the phrase 'the whole church' (Rom 16:23; 1 Cor 14:23) implies that on occasions the various house churches from across the city might well have met together for larger celebrations or events.

LEADERSHIP IN THE CHURCH

No clear blueprint for the structure of church leadership can be found in the New Testament.

The primary emphasis is on the members of the Church ministering to 'one another.'

Even so, some forms of leadership were necessary and are apparent.

- Its shape, together with the titles given to leaders, seems to have varied according to the situation.
- As with so much else in the New Testament, flexibility – rather than fixedness – seems characteristic.
- Among the leaders are apostles, deacons, elders or bishops and apostolic messengers.
- Prophets and teachers also seem to have leadership roles, perhaps with pastors and evangelists (Eph 4:11,12).

More concern is shown about the principles of leadership rather than the structure of leadership:–

- leaders are servants (Mark 10:35–45; John 13:1–17; 1 Pet 5:2–3).
- leaders are team-players – not Lone Rangers (3 John 9).
- leaders are to be spiritually qualified (1 Tim 3:1–10; Titus 1:5–9).
- leaders are accountable (1 Cor 4:1–5; Heb 7:17).
- leaders are set apart or recognised (Acts 13:1–3; 2 Tim 1:6).
- leaders are worthy of respect (1 Thess 5:12; 1 Tim 5:17).

THE MISSION OF THE CHURCH

The Church's primary calling was to be a people set apart for God. They were to be occupied with their calling as a royal priesthood. So they were to be about:–

- Worship.
- Intercession.
- Instruction.

Eph 4:11,12
It was he who gave some to be apostles, some to be prophets, some to be evangelists, and some to be pastors and teachers, to prepare God's people for works of service, so that the body of Christ may be built up.

- Personal purity.

This was not an agenda which was to make them concerned with their own affairs and inward looking.

That would misunderstand the priestly role. They had responsibilities beyond their own boundaries.
- They were to 'become blameless and pure, children of God without fault in a crooked and depraved generation, *in which you shine like stars in the universe as you hold out the word of life...*' (Phil 2:15–16).
- Their agendas were to be pursued for the sake of the world and the gospel.

Paul only speaks once of his own role as a priest – when talking of 'the priestly duty of proclaiming the gospel of God, so that the Gentiles might become an offering acceptable to God, sanctified by the Holy Spirit' (Rom 15:16).

Being a priest is no 'in-house role'. It is a role that exists to serve the world. It includes becoming living sacrifices (Rom 12:1,2) that we might be pleasing to God.

In this way the Early Church not only engaged with wider society but profoundly revolutionised it – turning the world upside down for Christ (Acts 17).

Romans 12:1,2
Therefore, I urge you, brothers, in view of God's mercy, to offer your bodies as living sacrifices, holy and pleasing to God – this is your spiritual act of worship. Do not conform any longer to the pattern of this world, but be transformed by the renewing of your mind. Then you will be able to test and approve what God's will is – his good, pleasing and perfect will.

1
2
3
4
5
6
7
8
9
10
11
12
13
14
15
16
17
18
19
20
21
22
23
24
25
26
27
28
29
30
31
32
33
34
35
36
37
38
39
40
41
42
43
44
45
46
47

THE CHALLENGES WE FACE AS A CHURCH

THE BIG PICTURE

The decline of the Church in Western countries raises serious new challenges for the UK church:–

- We shall need to strategically target evangelism and church planting efforts to reach those people under 35.
- We shall need to free up much more time and money among our members – to grow the Church into the third millennium and to expand mission to the growing needs of the poor here and overseas.
- With the escalating pressures facing families and singles, it will be increasingly essential to provide cell group and small groups for mutual support and accountability.
- As economic pressures mount, it will be increasingly essential to create new forms of mutual cooperation, including less expensive housing for the young and the poor.

Agents for transformation

At the local level, many Christians become involved at a handout level – opening soup kitchens or day-care centres. But there is far greater need for projects that transform the community itself – encouraging and helping its people to become all God intends them to be.

There is a role to Christians to play in facilitating the change in their local communities.

There is also a need to continue to explore new ways in which believers and non-believers alike can be drawn into community development projects as a means to bring the transforming influence of Christ to bear in their lives and in the lives of those around.

Centres of Celebration

In the context of an ever increasing multi-cultural community, the Church has much to offer.

For example:– The Icthus Fellowship in London has a richly multicultural congregation that celebrates many different and diverse cultural heritages. The fellowship has also started initiatives that recognise the specific needs of immigrants from other cultures. One such project is Pecan – a bold and creative response to unemployment.

In 1996, Pecan's team were named "Londoners of the Year" by London Electricity.

"It is no longer adequate for the Church to talk a good gospel from within the walls of stone buildings or in big mission events without the evidence of it being presented before the eyes of a hungry world. We must live lifestyles that back up our words, that release the power of God through the very actions we take," Andy Harrington writes in "Reaching a New Generation."

FACTS

Based in Peckham, the Pecan project helps people get jobs by:–
- assisting clients to build their self-confidence.
- teaching them to present themselves to potential employers.
- providing a special employment preparation course for those suffering from mental illness.
- teaching English as a second language and providing one-to-one literary support.

Places of refuge

The best antidote to worry and stress is to feel well-supported by other people. In this respect, churches have so much to offer society affected by change. Churches where people are noticed, cared for and given the opportunity to serve will provide that support. They will help people to feel secure in a world that is full of insecurities.

Fellowship could be one of God's biggest gifts to a frightened world over the next 20 years.

A new emphasis on mission

Involvement in global mission as a life vocation is on the decrease. This is a time when the number of those in the Two-Thirds World who need to be reached is projected to increase. This challenges us to be part of the solution.

SHORT-TERM MISSIONS

One response is a greater commitment to short-term missions. Such expeditions properly planned and executed – are a wonderful opportunity to develop Christians disciples, particularly young leaders.

The fact that many local churches are now planning their own overseas projects means many international mission organisations may need to take on a new role helping design mission trips for local churches and youth groups.

Statistics show that those who begin in short-term missions:–
- Are more likely to give long-term to overseas mission projects,
- Usually become more committed to church life and local mission.

A growing number of churches are recognising the potential of such experiences and are integrating short-term mission trips into discipleship programmes.

Following a short-term trip, participants are encouraged and helped to re-evaluate their lives and set some long-term goals. These relate to simplified living, sharing of resources and long-term involvement in mission projects overseas or in the local community.

New international partnerships

Another need is to encourage partnership between churches in the UK and in the Two-Thirds World. These relationships must be based on belief that we have as much to learn from Christians of other cultures as we have to teach, and at times, more.

Community-based approaches to ministry initiated in India or Africa may have tremendous application back in the UK.

One of the greatest untapped resources of the Church is the wealth of knowledge that returning missionaries bring with them.

In the West we struggle with the issues raised by the emergence of other religions besides Christianity in their society. Yet a believer in Sri Lanka would tell us, "We have been faced with a plurality of gods in our society for 2,000 years. There is much that we could teach you Westerners about interacting with other faiths."

A commitment to the environment

Environmental issues have not been a traditional area of concern among many Western Christians. However, as stewards of God's creation, we have a responsibility. The reawakening interest in Celtic Christianity has helped to highlight God's love of creation. The Celtic Christians regarded creation as sacred. Monks often portrayed a special affinity for animals and God's creation.

The BSE scandal has highlighted that the way we feed our animals and process our food can contribute to serious illness.
- The overuse of antibiotics in animals has greatly enhanced the spread of toxic organisms such as E coli and salmonella.
- In the future, there is likely to be growing concern about the quality of our food.

Expressing Justice

A concern for justice should turn our attention to the unfair trading practices that penalises those at the margins or on the bottom rungs of the ladder.

Churches can educate their people regarding:–
- the need for responsible shopping.
- the purchase of goods from fair trade organizations.

There is a growing need for education as new issues become clear and need a response.

For example, Europeans who have overfished the

1 North Sea are looking for new sources of supply.
2 Recently they discovered fish-rich Lake Victoria, which
3 has fed its surrounding 1 million people for centuries.
4
5 Fish factories have been built on the lake, paying top
6 price for the local produce and processing about 200
7 tons per week of fish for the European market.
8
9 Local inhabitants can no longer afford the high prices
10 and now buy bones and fish heads from the factories
11 to add a meagre amount of protein to their diets.
12
13 **Dynamic Relationships**
14 Jesus commands Christians to, "Be perfect … as your
15 heavenly Father is perfect" (Matt 5:48). The Early
16 Church understood this to mean to be perfected in
17 love.
18
19 It is God's desire that human society should also be
20 perfected in love. So the genuine, God given,
21 differences between human beings are respected, in a
22 context of mutual support.
23
24 One of the ways God is bringing this about is by the
25 work of the Church, which is:–
26 ● God's visual aid to the world as to the way in
27 which social relationships should be organised.
28 ● God's call to be different as they exercise a
29 prophetic ministry to the world at large.
30
31 The world cannot be expected to listen to our call for
32 repentance if they do not see the difference such
33 repentance makes. And they cannot be expected to see
34 the difference it can make if we will not speak out as
35 well as live it out.
36
37
38
39
40
41
42
43
44
45
46
47

THE FAMILY

THE FUTURE OF FAMILIES

What do we mean by 'Family'?

One of the biggest hot potatoes of the moment is the definition of 'family'. What it cannot exclusively mean is:–

- the traditional unit of a married couple with children.
- a group, commonly known as a 'household'.
- an ad hoc group without blood links or legal ties who are living under the same roof.

The definition of 'family' must include:–

- extended families with grandparents, aunts, uncles, etc.
- the many who are singles and genuinely part of a family, whether or not they have children of their own.

The place of unconditional love

Mum lies on the bed, perched against the pillows. An exhausted but warm glow fills her face.

Dad sits by her side, eyes fixed on the new arrival in his arms. It is a moment of family bliss, the child loved for all she is worth.

The newborn one has done nothing except arrive. The love for her is completely unconditional, given without expecting anything in return.

The future of unconditional love

Above everything else, what people probably long for from their families is unconditional love. This is:–

- **A love that makes us feel wanted** – giving a sense that we matter just because we exist, without first having to prove our worth.
- **A love that can heal the pain of rejection** – because we feel accepted as we are.
- **A love which makes us feel stronger inside** – giving us the confidence to learn and explore.

Never has this kind of love been more important. For adults, over the next 20 years friendships outside work will be at a premium.

The Henley Centre expects that: "By 2020, it will not be uncommon for first time mothers to be in their late 40s."

40

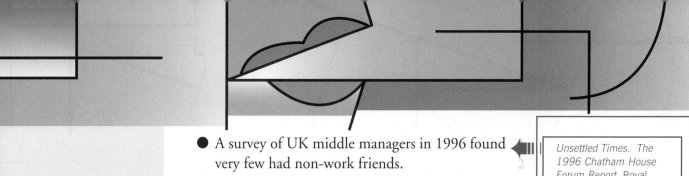

- A survey of UK middle managers in 1996 found very few had non-work friends.
- Almost one in ten fewer mothers of children under 16 were in weekly contact with their own mothers in 1995 compared to 10 years earlier (50% against 59%).
- More people are feeling lonely when arriving home from work.

This trend for people to need friends and living relationships will continue as:–

- Demands of work go on escalating.
- More people move further away from their families.
- The number of people who are lonely will grow.
- People will value their friends more highly, especially those they know intimately.
- If they have a partner, they will have high expectations of that relationship. They will want unconditional love.

The ability to relate closely with others will be increasingly prized – especially at work. As the UK economy becomes increasingly complex, people will spend more of their time in teams, networking with customers, suppliers and experts, and in meetings.

Getting on with other people will be increasingly recognised as the key to success.

Tomorrow's thriving economies will demand adults who relate well to others because they have been unconditionally loved themselves.

Barriers to Love

Frequently, work will continue to take precedence over the family.

Families of the future will find it harder to provide unconditional love.

A 1997 survey found that a quarter of British 15- and 16-year-olds think a happy family life will be the most important thing when they grow up. One-third put an interesting job first.

This indicates work-obsessed parents leaving children

Unsettled Times. The 1996 Chatham House Forum Report, Royal Institute of International Affairs, 1996, p.54.

"Young parents' contact with their relatives", *Findings,* Joseph Rowntree Foundation, May 1998.

Survey results available from Media Research Group, London School of Economics.

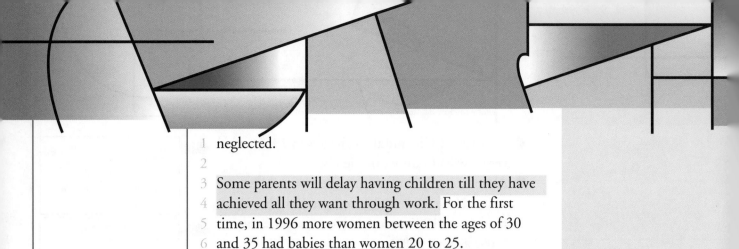

1   neglected.

2

3   Some parents will delay having children till they have
4   achieved all they want through work. For the first
5   time, in 1996 more women between the ages of 30
6   and 35 had babies than women 20 to 25.

7

The Sunday Times, 9 November 1997, News, p. 3.

  Harvard scientists are confident of developing a
9   technique to enable high-flying women to delay
10   having children till their late 40s or 50s.

11

12   The late child will become a 'project'.

13   ● Parents' schedules will be built entirely around
        their children – signing them up for all kinds of

Next Generation. Lifestyles for the future, The Henley Centre, 1998, p. 16.

15   activities and hobbies so that they shine from an
16   early age.
17   ● Love will be expressed by getting the child to do
18   things.
19   ● Parents will feel exhausted, while children may
20   feel loved only for what they achieve rather than
21   for who they are.

22

23

24

FACTS

Percent of people saying that social skills were increasing or decreasing in their job, between 1992 and 1997

Skill Type	% Increasing	% Decreasing
Dealing with people	34.7	12.6
Instructing, training or teaching people	46.7	17.3
Making speeches or presentations	31.9	12.4
Persuading or influencing others	36.4	21.8
Selling a product or service	29.4	20.1
Counselling, advising or caring for customers or clients	36.9	24.6
Working with a team of people	34.9	27.8

Source: Francis Green et al, *"Are British Workers Getting More Skilled?"* in A.B.Atkinson & John Hills (eds), *Exclusion, Employment and Opportunity*, London School of Economics, 1998, p. 118.

36

37   Babies will increasingly be made to order.

38

39   Developments in birth control, in-vitro fertilisation
40   and genetics will give parents:–
41   ● a much greater control over human
42   reproduction.
43   ● a greater say over when the baby arrives.

44

45   Genetic therapies will treat genes in the foetus where
46   there is a risk of serious physical disease. This may
47   extend to some emotional disorders.

This will mean:–
- advantages in terms of disease control
- the notion of unconditional love seeming strange. "You've turned out the way we want and we love you" is very different to, "You've arrived and we love you the way you are."

Children will increasingly be the commercial product of their school.

A child's grades and results will matter more than their personal development. Because this is the measure that will attract the future intake and greater funding.

Children will have less confidence to make a go of their lives.

Two-thirds of the variations in 16-year-olds' GCSE results reflect differences in deprivation. Those from poorer families do less well.

Richard G. Wilkinson, *Unhealthy Societies*, Routledge, 1996, p. 165.

Almost a third of under fives were in families drawing Income Support in 1993. So in less than fifteen years' time the experience of poverty will have shaped the lives of nearly a third of 20- to 25-year-olds.

Patricia Morgan, *Farewell to the Family*, IEA, 1995, p. 29.

These and other developments will make it more difficult for families to be havens of unconditional love. At the very time when this love will be in greatest demand, families will be least able to show it.

1
2
3
4
5
6
7
8
9
10
11
12
13
14
15
16
17
18
19
20
21
22
23
24
25
26
27
28
29
30
31
32
33
34
35
36
37
38
39
40
41
42
43
44
45
46
47

THE FUTURE OF PARENTING

The number of births to women of childbearing age – the fertility rate – has been falling in recent years (see table below). The trend is likely to continue.

Almost a fifth of women born since 1960 are predicted to remain voluntarily childless, partly because they value careers over motherhood. By 2010 this could be up to almost a third.

A 1997 study by the Office of National Statistics found the number of couples who have decided to have only one child has risen by nearly a half to 2.9 million.

Lone parents now head almost a quarter of families with children – nearly three times the proportion in 1971.

Helen Wilkinson &
Melanie Howard et al,
Tomorrow's Women,
Demos, 1997, p. 103.

FACTS

Fertility Rate

Women aged today	Average no. of children per woman
59	2.36
54	2.19
44	1.99

Source: Lynda Clarke, *"Demographic Change and the Family Situation of Children"* in Julia Brannen & Margaret O'Brien (eds), Children in Families: Research and Policy, Falmer, 1996, pp. 70–1.

HOW COULD IT TURN OUT?

The future of parenting and the future of marriage, each offering two alternative scenarios. These scenarios do not predict the future. They just help us think about what could be in twenty years time.

Scenario 1 – Society shares the load

Society will adapt to the pressures on parents by sharing the load. An African proverb says, "It takes a village to raise a child."

This trend has already begun:–

- The Government aims to have after-school

home-work clubs in half of all secondary schools and a quarter of primary schools by the next election.
- Already there are more nannies in Britain than carworkers.

In twenty years time, child supervision by non-parents will start earlier in the child's life and cover a longer part of the day. In effect there will be an extension of schooling, but in a varied way.

So there will be:–
- More child minders, workplace nurseries, preschool education and after-school home-work clubs.
- Saturday cyber clubs where children can mix and match home-work with computer games and chatting to friends.

Steps will be taken to raise the quality of parenting. We shall see:–
- Parent-school contracts introduced, making clear what parents can expect of school and what the school expects from parents. This is to encourage parents to take greater responsibility for their children's education.
- New legislation that requires parents to take parenting classes if their children continually break legal orders – such as to attend school.
- Parenting classes formally integrated into post-natal care. They could also be run by schools to help parents fulfil their side of parent-school contracts.
- Child Benefit made conditional on attending parenting classes at key stages of the child's development – after birth, when starting school and just before adolescence.
- Parenting become a professional activity for which training is required.

This scenario offers more opportunities for churches:–
- To run playgroups, nurseries and other pre-school childcare services.
- To organise after-school clubs.
- To lay on parenting classes.
- To provide childcare facilities for shoppers at weekends.

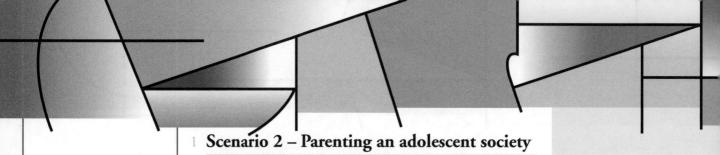

1 **Scenario 2 – Parenting an adolescent society**
2 Society will become 'adolescent' due to 20 years of
3 adults who have been poorly parented. This scenario is
4 not inconsistent with the previous one. Adults will:–
5 ● Behave like perpetual adolescents, because they
6 will have been deprived of parental love.
7 ● Constantly crave a good time – to bury the
8 uncomfortable feelings they have about
9 themselves.
10 ● Crave the approval of their peers due to personal
11 insecurity.
12 ● Want everything now – being too anxious to
13 delay gratification.
14 ● Keep pushing against the traditional boundaries
15 of morality.
16 ● Turn to drugs – Prozac and others – to feel
17 better.
18
19
20

QUESTION ?

In the light of this scenario, could
churches do more to:–
● Work with local schools to provide a counselling service
for parents who want help.
● Cooperate with GP's surgeries to provide counselling,
bereavement and spiritual advice services.
● Mentor people at work so that they behave ethically and
manage stress.
● Strengthen the reputation of their healing ministries, for
example by developing recognised codes that enshrine
best practice.

30
31 To cope, these 'adolescent adults' will need the
32 equivalent of parents:–
33 ● To act as role models.
34 ● To help them come to terms with reality and to
35 set boundaries.
36
37 These 'parents' will be found in a whole range of
38 experts who will help them relate to other adults, as
39 well as to their own children. These experts will make
40 up for the lack of parenting the adults received as
41 children.
42
43 They will include:–
44 ● Mentors
45 ● Facilitators
46 ● Spiritual guides
47 ● Counsellors and listeners of various description.

This trend in adult parenting has already started. There is a growing use of facilitators in the workplace – to manage meetings to help groups reach agreement

The concept of 'coaching' – which has taken off in the United States – is spreading to Britain.

Within twenty years some may have a network of 'coaches.'
- A facilitator for group meetings.
- A mentor for work relationships.
- A spiritual guide to improve a sense of well-being.
- A counsellor to help with a 'difficult' child.

The person who is a chair of School Governors may have a further mentor as a guide through the increasingly dense jungle of local, regional, national and European government.

These advisers may know their 'children' well and be so committed to them they become almost extended family members. They could have the kind of quality we normally associate with relatives.

THE FUTURE OF MARRIAGE

The traditional pattern of courtship followed by marriage "till death do us part" has now given way to more varied patterns of coupling.

- Of women marrying in the late 1960s, only just over one in twenty were already living together. By the late '80s the figure was almost twelve in twenty. And the trend is still rising.
- Four in ten new marriages now end in divorce.
- Of those who remarry, seven out of ten couples had lived together.
- Cohabiting has replaced marriage in the early years of the relationship. And is the norm for couples where at least one partner is between marriages.
- Nine out of ten people whose marriages break down go on to live with someone else.

These trends are likely to continue.

- The more alternatives there are to marriage, the less compelling marriage will feel.
- This present choice-driven culture will be reinforced by the gradual spread of tailor-made attitudes (see Society – Page 63 onwards). This will continue to weaken commitment to marriage. People will feel more able to quit if they are unhappy; "It's my decision."
- Women will continue to be less financially dependent on their partners, making it easier to separate if they wish.

THE WAY IT MAY TURN OUT

There are two possible ways things might look in the future.

Scenario 1– A cohabitation/marriage

People will both seek long-term if not permanent relationships, accepting that often relationships do not work out.

To reflect this tension, commitment will continue to be redefined in terms of the present; "I hope this

Jonathan Bradshaw, "Family Policy and Family Poverty", *Policy Studies,* 17 (2), 1996,pp. 94-5.

Nick Nuttall, "Five reasons why official housing figures may be wrong", T*he Times,* 26 January 1998, p. 8.

relationship will last. I don't know if it will. But I will be totally committed to you while it does. I won't sleep with anyone else while I am sleeping with you."

As a result:–
- The compromise between the ideal of permanence and the frequent reality of divorce and separation will encourage more couples to cohabit for longer.
- Cohabitation will combine a here-and-now commitment, often in the hope that the relationship will become permanent, with a recognition that this may not be the case.

To reflect this compromise, cohabitees may be allowed to register their union legally. If the couple breaks up:–
- They could apply to the court for a fair distribution of their joint possessions.
- The father might find it easier to secure rights over any children born to the couple.

Many cohabitees will eventually marry – as they do now. But a growing number may first enter into a prenuptial agreement. These agreements specify how possessions should be divided if they divorce.

The end result will be that cohabitation becomes more like marriage and marriage more like cohabitation.
- Cohabitation will have a legal framework that brings it closer to marriage.
- More couples starting marriage will prepare for its possible failure in advance.
- Commitment will be combined with the prospect of impermanence.

Scenario 2 – Home Alone
Singleness will become more common, though long-term coupling will remain important.

The trend in singleness is accelerating.
- In 1971, slightly less than one in five of all English households contained a single person.

Social Trends.

- By 1991 this had risen to just over one in four.
- By 2016 it is predicted to reach more than one in three.
- By 2020, approaching four out of ten English homes could be single. Many of these will be

49

older people, but by no means all.

For a growing number of people, adult singleness will not be a transitional stage before or between coupling. It will become the norm.

These singles will:–
- look for intimacy with a variety of people.
- be reluctant to make a long-term commitment to any one.

This trend could be driven by our ever faster global economy. With many people absorbed in their work and travel:–
- They may be unwilling to be tied down.
- They will prefer flexible relationships to fit in with their flexible work.
- The spread of tailor-made values may encourage ever higher expectations of relationships. "They must fit me exactly."

Because relationships often do not fit us exactly, there has to be give and take on both sides. People may become disillusioned and give up on their partner more quickly than today. Or they may prefer a greater variety of intimate relationships, taking one thing from this relationship and something different from another.

The growing number of single households will have a huge impact on society.

A massive building programme is needed to house the extra people who will want to live on their own. The official government forecast is that an extra 4.4 million new homes will have to be built before 2016.

This is a land area roughly equivalent to the size of greater London. Where will these new homes be built, and what will they do to the environment?

People living on their own, except perhaps the very old, will not want to stay indoors every evening.

People will want to be out with friends in restaurants, pubs and cinemas. Or leisure *canapés* – to spend three hours dipping in and out of food courts, bowling alleys, video games or evening classes.

GOD'S GOOD INTENTIONS FOR FAMILIES

FAMILIES ARE RELATIONSHIPS

Families are the created context for growing into relationship. They are based on the central meaning of relationships – unconditional love.

Children give their love of parents a tangible fleshly form. From the beginning a child has relationships with two parents, learning to depend on the relationship they have with one another.

This family relationship should be a place of peace and goodness where the child is cradled in the love of father and mother. As the psalmist says: "But I have stilled and quietened my soul; like a weaned child with its mother, ..." (Psa 131:2).

What God intended for the family is close to the meaning of life.

The created structure of family is the first community of life. Paul talks (Eph 3) about our confidence in coming to God and says how our lives should be rooted and grounded in love. In the middle of this thought he throws in a breathtaking sentence: "For this reason I kneel before the Father, from whom his whole family in heaven and earth derives its name" (Eph 3:14).

This verse is not entirely clear, but seems to imply that:–

- Just as God is Creator, so mother and father are procreators.
- As God gives unconditional love, so mother and father are called to give love.
- We are born into relationships which draw their meaning from God the loving Father.

Psa 131:2
"But I have stilled and quietened my soul; like a weaned child with its mother, ..."

Eph 3:14
"For this reason I kneel before the Father, from whom his whole family in heaven and earth derives its name."

Relationships are God's idea

Relationships have an important structure that is mirrored in the family.

People are not called to own one another, or control one another, but to live in neighbour love with one another.

The two great commandments are linked. We love God and live our lives before God. Consequently we love our neighbour as ourselves. Each person's identity comes from God. We are God's and he has made us – parent and child. We are his people – parent and child (Psa 100:3).

So parents:–
- Do not own their children or control them.
- Are given care of their children.
- Are to live alongside them before God, allowing them to grow to maturity from dependence.

Families are not mechanisms of control, but formative communities where good relationships are learnt.

Parents are to be honoured

The first of the Ten Commandments to come after those relating to God is: "Honour your father and your mother, ..."
- Parents are the adults we have been given for our nurture.
- We have grown through their care and love.
- They have made a unique contribution to who we are.

This love and care – and the returned honour to the parents – are basic to human life.

There is no substitute for it. The basic meaning of a home is the love and relationships within it. Not who pays for what. For these relationships to have integrity, other things need to give them space to develop.

Crucial are:–
- Time together.
- Focussed attention.
- Open communication.
- Unconditional love.

Christian Families

Christian love expressed in families is not meant to be self-centred.

Real love never can be self-centred. Paul says: "Each of you should look not only to your own interests, but also to the interests of others" (Phil 2:4).

There are two kinds of families which create problems:–
- the parent-centred family.
- the child-centred family.

Both allow self-importance. Parents can use children, and want returns from them – "After all I've done for you". Such selfishness can undermine the children's life. Children can also be spoiled and not taught a proper regard and care for others. Spoiling children often stems from parental guilt. It leaves the child weak in the long run.

THE GOD-CENTRED FAMILY

The central pattern of family life is where both parents and children live in faith and obedience before God.

Parenting

It takes two – ideally. Throughout the Bible equal significance in loving and bringing up children is given to both father and mother. There is no suggestion of passive fathering, or of this being mainly the mother's role.

In Ephesians and Colossians, Paul draws special attention to the attitude of fathers.
- "Fathers, do not exasperate your children; instead, bring them up in the training and instruction of the Lord." (Eph 6:4).

And:–
- "Fathers, do not embitter your children, or they will become discouraged." (Col 3:21).

This shows the commitment fathers, as well as mothers, should have. Fathers should be as fully involved in parenting as mothers.

The biblical and biological norm is for two parents – a mother and father in marriage. This gives a child:–

- economic and practical support.
- male and female characteristics to relate to.
- the model of a marriage relationship from which the child can learn.
- no one person as focus in their lives.
- parents who depend on their marriage partner for love and not the child.
- variety and richness.
- parents who can cope by sharing.

While the norm is two parents, sometimes things work out differently.

When it does, single parents are to be honoured – because of the important task they are undertaking, under even more difficult circumstances.

The Christian Dimension

Christian parenting involves giving to our children in the same way as God the Father gives to us.

Our attitudes are important – patience, love, respect, kindness and gentleness. Jesus adds other dimensions:–

- We are to welcome children, not exclude them.
- Because children are dependent on us, it is possible to cause them to sin – by provoking them. And so causing them to be violent, selfish, and lose self-control. This must not be done.
- The faith our children have in God is to be honoured.

Parenting involves education and discipline.

In the Old Testament, God's law was to be read and taught to children (Deut 6). Most education happens in the home mainly through what is seen and experienced.

Children have wonderful abilities to learn about God to relate to him personally and become wise.

Bringing children to maturity involves:–

- perseverence (Heb 10:19–39).
- discipline, learning to live in good ways (Heb 12).

- developing in our own relationship with God (1 Cor 2).
- learning to allow love – a commitment to the best for others – to shape our lives and relationships (1 Cor 13).
- being realistic about our sin (1 John 1).
- testing and strengthening our faith (James 1:2–8).
- for Christians, helping children to grow in maturity towards God.

MARRIAGE AND COHABITATION

Marriage has an important created structure, which cannot be ignored.

It is a universal institution throughout human history. For it to be replaced by cohabitation is wrong.

Cohabitation involves various defective forms of the marriage relationship. While, sometimes, it is effectively marriage.

Marriage is meant to have the following characteristics:–
- It is instituted by God. Which means that people need to enter it on God's terms, not believe they can create their own.
- It is linked in with our relationship to God. God's love and faithfulness are the main guidelines to the meaning of marriage.
- It is not the central meaning of life. Nor are romantic love and sex, there is a danger of making them into an idol, etc.
- It is voluntary, mutual and requires maturity. Marriage or singleness are open choices.
- It is a public declaration – not a private agreement.
- It is heterosexual – for a man and woman – involved in sharing bodies, sex and potentially the procreation of children.
- It is monogamous – for one man and one woman – because you can only share your marital life fully with one partner.
- It is a union. A person shares all areas of their life with the other and receives all of the other

55

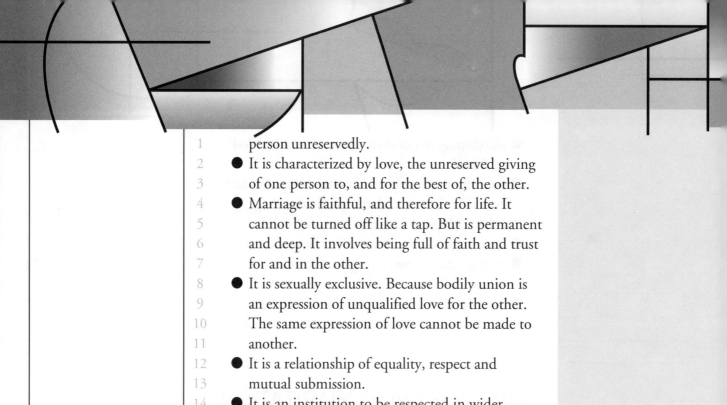

person unreservedly.

- It is characterized by love, the unreserved giving of one person to, and for the best of, the other.
- Marriage is faithful, and therefore for life. It cannot be turned off like a tap. But is permanent and deep. It involves being full of faith and trust for and in the other.
- It is sexually exclusive. Because bodily union is an expression of unqualified love for the other. The same expression of love cannot be made to another.
- It is a relationship of equality, respect and mutual submission.
- It is an institution to be respected in wider society, the law and the economy.

The created structure and meaning of marriage is expressed in Genesis: "For this reason a man will leave his father and mother and be united to his wife, and they will become one flesh" (Gen 2:24). It implies:–

- The importance of father and mother to the process of growing up.
- Maturity means moving from dependence on the family unit into full adult selfhood.
- It is wrong for parents to dominate the decisions and circumstances of their children's marriages.
- Marriage is a personal union without barriers of sharing.

Permanence in marriage has to do with faithfulness – a fruit of the Holy Spirit. Faithfulness is about being there for the other. Always protecting, trusting, hoping, persevering (1 Cor 13:7).

A family with Christ at its centre is a microcosm of the Church:–

- Love and relationships are at its heart.
- Others see the glory of Jesus expressed through it.
- The needs of others are met by it.

THE CHALLENGES WE FACE AS FAMILIES

Our rapidly changing world places growing stress on all our lives. Especially on the integrity of families and other important relationships.

- Families whose members are Christians are just as prone to the impact of change as those who are not.
- Young people who are Christians can feel the added pressures of the demands for excellence in their academic leisure and moral lives. The result is an ever increasing burden.

Christian parents have a responsibility to prepare their children:–

- To live in a more complex future in which the population will be aging and much more racially blended than today.
- To steward the new technologies in a way that will honor God and advance God's kingdom.
- To be much more serious disciples and better stewards of their resources.

Church leadership can prepare its families and singles:–

- To live in a world in which pressures on their budgets and their time schedules are likely to increase.
- To relate their faith and what they hear in church to what they do with their lives the rest of the week.
- To create their own mission statements that reflect God's purposes for their life – equipping them to be stewards of their life and so re-order their time and resources in line with their goals.
- To enable people to free up more time to develop their spiritual lives and for serving the growing needs in the community.
- To celebrate the kingdom seven days a week.
- To prepare a new generation of disciples with a clear understanding of God's purposes for their

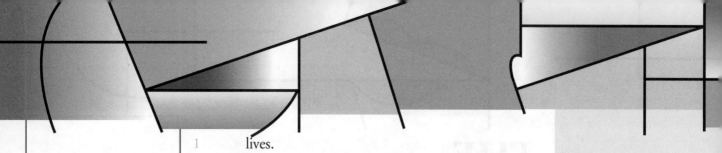

lives.

- To prepare a new generation who will act as God's agents for change in the new millennium.

What can your family do together? What acts of Christian service can you do together as a family? Finding something and doing it:–

- Strengthens family bonds.
- Provides a challenging witness to those who see their parents living out their faith in practical ways.

Families for Singles?

The rapid growth of the singles population raises unique challenges for the church.

There is a great need for the re-introduction of extended families. Places where singles feel welcomed:–

- Not just as a means to raise extra finances by renting rooms or as an extra baby sitter.
- But as an important part of the social framework of the family.

The Bible teaches that the local church is intended to be a family. Jesus did not in any way downplay the importance of biological family. But he drew a new circle that also included all of us in the Body of Christ as family.

*Andy Harrington, leader of Synergy, Ground Level's national youth network, says: "Young people no longer want to be **told** the truth; they want to be **shown** the truth. We must live lifestyles that back up our words and release the power of God through the very actions that we take."*

SOCIETY

THE FUTURE OF SOCIETY

AN ANXIOUS WORLD

When people think about the future, they often do so with fear, even alarm. We live in anxious times, and these anxieties are likely to continue.

Global competition is making it harder for firms to keep ahead.

The speed of communications and developments in technology means new product developments or management practices can be copied within almost a few months. A company which innovates and jumps ahead hardly has time to make a profit on its investment before its rivals catch up.

The pace becomes ever more frantic as more firms plug into the global economy and information is exchanged worldwide in nanoseconds. With the cost of computer power halving every 18 months, this bewildering speed of change will continue in overdrive.

People will feel more stressed at work.

The number of people who feel secure in their job plummeted from three-quarters in 1990 to less than half in 1996.

Most workers are spending almost as long with the same employer now as they were 20 years ago. But more people are on short-term contracts, so there is no guarantee their jobs will continue.

This trend is set to remain a feature of working life. A survey of 5,000 women found more than one in three took at least nine days off work in 1997 because of stress. Research shows the main reason for workplace stress is feeling you are not in control of your work and lack support from other people.

The growth of workplace anxiety and stress will increase due to:–
- ● The information glut spreading "information

The Henley Centre, *2020 Vision*, 1998, p. 29. Simon Burgess & Hedley

Rees, "A disaggregate analysis of the evolution of job tenure in Britain, 1975-93", Centre for Economic Policy Research, Discussion Paper Series, No. 1711, 1997.

The Times, 14 July 1997

fatigue syndrome"
- The greater monitoring of people's work performance
- The "virtual office" leading to people travelling more, spending more time at home and networking round a wider range of contacts, ending up having fewer close colleagues to provide emotional support.

A survey in 1994 revealed that nearly one in six UK employees had been in their present job for less than a year, and half for fewer than five years. In addition:–
- The number of self-employed workers in the UK has increased from just over 2 million in 1971 to almost 3.4 million in 1994 – an increase of almost 70 per cent.
- In the past ten years the number of people working 50 hours or more a week has risen to more than one in five of the workforce – an increase of 40 per cent.
- The average British lunch-hour is now 30 minutes.
- Seven out of ten British workers want to work only 40 hours a week but only three out of ten do so.
- More than one in ten out of the workforce – almost 2.5 million people – have no annual paid leave.

Quoted in *Pressure Points*, Word UK, by Peter Meadows.

People will feel increasingly busy.

A MORI survey in 1997 found about half of full-time employees in Britain thought that they were working such long hours they had too little time for their families. At the same time, parents are spending more time ferrying children from music to drama to an assortment of friends. These demands will increase as society becomes more affluent, provides more opportunities for children and is perceived as less safe. In an ageing society, adults will have to make time for children, grandchildren, and elderly relatives as well. More people will feel anxious because they are so busy.

People will face information overload.

Today's technology makes generating and storing large quantities of information even easier.

The integrated circuit, invented only in the late 1950s, permits ever-increasing volumes of information to be processed or stored on a single micro-chip.

As a result, more information has been produced in the past 30 years than during the previous 5,000:–
- Twenty-five years ago, there were fewer than 25,000 computers on the planet.
- Today there are more than 200 million.
- The information supply doubles every five years.

A study found that:–
- The average middle-management executive sends or receives 178 messages and documents each day.
- Secretarial staff face more than 190 daily correspondences, including post, e-mail, faxes, phone calls, voice-mail, sticky notes, pager messages, courier deliveries and internet mail.
- More than seven out of ten managers feel overwhelmed by their correspondence.

An independent, international survey published by Reuters Business Information leaves no doubt this excess of information causes widespread mental anguish and physical illness.

Growing old will be worrying for many more people.

In 1995 there were less than 9 million people over 65 in the UK.
- By 2030 there will be half as many again – almost 14 million.
- At least a third will have to rely on the basic state pension, which today is worth a meagre sixth of average male earnings.
- The value of pensions is likely to fall in real terms, and many will feel financially insecure.

Food scares and other environmental concerns will persist.

Planet-wide issues, such as global warming, will continue to provide a background of disease. While experts agree that the risk of an upturn in infectious diseases is growing.

Quoted in *Pressure Points*, Word UK, by Peter Meadows.

Communications Overload, by Gallup and the Institute for the Future.

Government Actuary's mid-1994 based principal projections, reproduced in Debate of the Age, *Paying for Age*, 1998, p.7.

Jerome C. Glenn & Theodore J. Gordon (eds), *1997 State of the Future*, American Council for the United Nations University, 1997, p. 3.

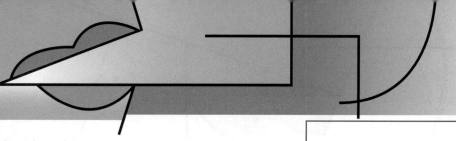

Already there have been:–
- Outbreaks of bubonic plague in India;
- The spread of the ebola virus in Africa;
- The emergence of drug-resistant strains of tuberculosis in the USA.

Some experts fear there could be a window when resistance to antibiotics builds up but new antibiotics have not been developed. This would allow infectious diseases that had been under control to return with a vengeance.

Other concerns will be about the long-term effects of genetically modified food, or whether we have the wisdom to responsibly use advances in human genetics.

The anxiety of the second consumer revolution

A new consumer revolution will generate greater levels of anxiety and stress through over-choice.

The first consumer revolution was pioneered in the United States between the two world wars. It swept through western Europe in the 1950s and involved:–
- Mass production on an unprecedented scale;
- A whole range of products became available at prices that the ordinary person could afford;
- The supermarket was born.

The result was the off-the-peg society. Any large supermarket offered 10,000 product lines and goods and services were mass-produced for a mass of customers.

This in itself created anxiety due to over-choice. For example, in the mid-1970s, the average American supermarket offered the choice of some 9,000 items. By 1985 it was 22,000.

Today it is more than 50,000. Clark claims that one month alone saw 235 new items launched on the American market. It seems that the UK is not far behind – if *behind* is the right word.

This is going to get even worse with the arrival of a new tailor-made society.

At Custom Foot, Connecticut, sales assistants use a digital foot imager to take customers' exact measurement. The customer chooses from a variety of designs – differently shaped heels and toes and different colours of leather.
The final specifications are sent electronically to Italy where the shoes are made and dispatched to the customer's home. The results are shoes that are exactly the right fit, tailor-made to personal style.

James H. Gilmore & B. Joseph Pine 11, "The Four Faces of Mass Customization", Harvard Business Review, Jan.-Feb. 1997, pp.91-101.

The Want Makers, Eric Clark

1 The introduction of digital TV and shopping on the
2 internet are just part of a move to a tailor-made
3 society. In this new world, what we buy and how it is
4 delivered will fit our individual taste and requirements.
5
6 Clothing industry experts predict customers will
7 increasingly design their own clothes:–
8   ● Using TV screens to assemble their designs from
9   a variety of patterns;
10   ● Choosing from a range of fabrics;
11   ● Having their measurements taken, so the
12   garment can be custom-made to their size and
13   taste.
14
15 At the Levi's store in London's Regent Street you can
16 record your own selection of songs from a computer
17 hard drive on to a blank CD. For £4.99 you come
18 away with a CD with your own unique combination
19 of tracks.
20
21 Manufacturers are talking about miniaturising food
22 processing plants so they will fit into supermarkets or
23 the corner shop. Pre-prepared meals will be stored on
24 site and the mini-plants will tailor these meals to the
25 customer's own tastes and needs. You could even avoid
26 ingredients to which you are allergic and cater for
27 other dietary requirements.
28
29 The delivery of what you buy will be tailor-made. A
30 host of experiments are under way to see how
31 electronic shopping can best be done. Experts predict a
32 whole variety of arrangements:–
33   ● People computer-shopping from work with
34   deliveries to the work-place;
35   ● Others ordering from home with deliveries to
36   the front door;
37   ● Ordering bulk goods from home or work and
38   collecting from drop-off points, such as garages;
39   ● Ordering some things on-line, going to the
40   supermarket to collect what they have ordered.
41
42 The age of hundreds of television channels is likely to
43 be short-lived. By 2020 several broadcasters will
44 probably offer the tailor-made delivery of a wide range
45 of programmes to download on to a built-in recorder
46 and to play at a time of our convenience.
47

The Guardian, 15 June 1998, p. 7.

Institute of Chemical Engineers, *Future Life: Engineering Solutions for the Next Generation,* London, 1997, pp. 24-5.

It will be common for rail tickets to include the price of a taxi to take you to and from the station, saving the time wasted looking for a car park or waiting for a bus. Hand-held personal information systems, the mobile phones of the future, will say when the next bus is due.

We may only subscribe to one broadcaster, trusted for its choice because it is designed for people like us. It may reflect certain religious or environmental values with which we identify.

This customisation may feel like a return to the days before the Industrial Revolution when goods were crafted to an individual's specific instructions.

But this tailor-made society will combine an individualised approach with low-cost mass production.

We shall have much more to choose from and at prices we can afford. What we buy will increasingly be designed to fit us exactly.

Everything tailor-made

Similar tailor-made trends will be true of almost every walk of life.

For instance, mass transport, like buses and rail, will be individualised to entice people off the roads.

Pension schemes will be personalised.

People will stop buying into a mass pension scheme managed on behalf of members as a whole. Many are already choosing their own particular mix of funds within the wider plan.

General Motors has 55 funds in its plan. Employees choose to have their investments managed for them or to do it themselves, with different levels of choice according to how sophisticated they want to be.

In 1998, GM conducted around 1,800 investment seminars to help its employees make more informed decisions about the options available.

USA Today, 27 August 1997, Section B, p. 3.

In education, students will learn at their own pace in ways that suit them best.

This will be achieved through new computer programmes and distance learning via the internet.

Individual Pressure

As we participate in the second consumer revolution, the concept of choice will be extended radically.

There will be an expectation that everything will be tailor-made. "It must fit me exactly" will be the defining outlook.

People won't want to keep up with the Joneses. They will want to be different from the Joneses.

This future puts more pressure on the individual:–
- There will be more decisions to take;
- The individual will be more responsible for them;
- There will be fewer close relationships to help us make decisions, or to support us when we get it wrong;
- There will be less time, due to the pace of life, to make the decisions.

What will be the outcome?
- Will these attitudes draw people together in mutual support, which could make life feel less anxious?
- Will they drive them apart so individuals feel even more alone in a threatening world?

HOW COULD IT TURN OUT?

Here are possible scenarios of the way things could turn out. They are not predictions of the future. They are simply designed to help us think about what the future could be like.

Scenario 1 – Fragmented Lives

Twenty-one years from now, we will live in personalised communities based on leisure and life-style interests.
- Old-fashioned communities of place – where we were born – will not have completely disappeared. But the tailor-made mentality will demand communities to fit the individual exactly.
- Like will gravitate to like. People will want to mix with others who share the same hobbies,

66

enjoy the same TV programmes, who are similar in age, outlook and so on.

This scenario is not so different to the lives of many people today. Individuals are involved in a variety of communities. Take Seth, for example:–

- He goes to the occasional meeting of Greenpeace and gives them an annual donation.
- He plays snooker every week with some friends.
- He stays behind on Friday evenings for a drink with his workmates.
- At home, via his computer, he exchanges jokes with friends all round the world, most of whom he has never met.
- Every fortnight he joins a group for transcendental meditation.

By belonging to a number of networks, Seth feels connected to other people.

This eases the pain of living in a high-risk society. Yet it is not entirely satisfying. In each group Seth is known mainly through the interests he shares with the others – his concern for the environment, his snooker, his shared experiences at work, his jokes and his desire to meditate.

Each group knows a part of Seth. But who can see him as a whole person? Perhaps that leads to an uncomfortable thought: "Would anyone accept the whole if they knew it?" And who values Seth for himself, rather than because they have an interest in common?

Compare: "We welcome you to this group because you share our interest in the protection of whales" with "We welcome you because you live in the neighbourhood."

The first is a statement about doing: "You are joining the cause."

The second is a statement about being: "You are welcome because you are here."

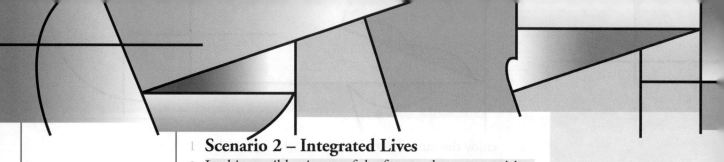

Scenario 2 – Integrated Lives

In this possible picture of the future, the communities that fit people exactly are increasingly the ones which integrate the different parts of each person.

Seth's ethical interests – the environment – were kept separate from his hobby – snooker – which was separate from his spiritual life – meditation – which was separate from friends with whom he swapped jokes.

By contrast, consider Mindi.

- She joins a religious sect which is campaigning against local prostitution. It consumes most of her time.
- She finds the different parts of herself are expressed in the one community.
- It is a leisure group, because she is involved in her spare time.
- There is work involved, though it is unpaid – planning, organising, taking action – which gives her a sense of achievement, a purpose, a structure for the weekend and the chance to make friends.
- The campaign allows the ethical side of her character to be expressed.
- The sect's worship gives expression to her spiritual dimension.

Mindi knows the people in her community much better than Seth knows the people he is involved with. This is because she spends more time with them and sees different aspects of their character.

She has a greater sense of being known, understood and accepted for whom she is. This helps her to come to terms with the anxieties of everyday life.

But she knows fewer people than Seth, and sometimes finds the relationships a little claustrophobic. If she had to move away from the area or the sect fell apart, in terms of friendships she would lose almost everything.

QUESTION ?

Whose shoes would you prefer to be in – Seth's or Mindi's? Why?

GOD'S GOOD INTENTIONS FOR SOCIETY

HONOURING GOD'S IMAGE

Human beings organise themselves in a variety of different ways, forming what we call society.
In every case, the common denominator is the individual.

To understand what God thinks about society we must first understand what he says about people.

Scripture affirms that people are made in the image of God (Gen 1:27). It is hard to be very precise about what that means. But the way we relate to people may be transformed if we recognise we are relating to those who image God for us – if we allow them to. There is a distinction between God and human beings – as Scripture makes clear (Is 46:9). But we still image God our creator.

This is reinforced by the fact that God became human himself. By doing so he hallowed the life which we often take for granted.

When God in Christ became human it was not only an act of solidarity with us. But also for our redemption.

The sanctity of human life is underlined by the fact that God has become human and died to save human beings. The New Testament goes further, pointing out that those who respond to this gospel receive the Holy Spirit of God himself.

So each human person – of every colour, shape, creed, and ability is:–
- made in God's image.
- redeemed by God Incarnate.
- and in whom the Holy Spirit longs to dwell.

This makes it hard to imagine how Christians have

ever been able to:–

- despise their fellow human beings,
- 'own' them as slaves,
- exploit them when children,
- sideline or subjugate them as women,
- hate and exterminate them as people of other races,
- neglect them as aged,
- destroy them with the weapons of mass destruction or debt or hunger.

This starting point gives us a basis as we think about how to plan and work for a society in which people are treated with respect and love, justice and mercy, for God's sake.

God and Society

God is interested in society and in social patterns. This can be seen from the way both the Old and New Testaments are ultimately concerned with human relationships of one kind or another.

In the creation narrative:–

- God is concerned that male-man should not be alone. So creates a complementary female-woman (Gen 2:18).
- With this companion, Adam is commanded to create family and society by procreation (Gen 1:28).
- Together, after their joint disobedience, the two are expelled from the immediate presence of God (Gen 3:23).
- At the end time, there is to be a city in which all the redeemed are gathered into the presence of God (Rev 21).
- This will be a community in which the reconciling work of Christ is completed (2 Cor 5). Nothing will break these relationships, hence there are to be no more tears.

Time began with all things in perfect harmony. And it will ultimately be that way for eternity.

Between these times, we live in a world in which we long for the promised Paradise. But we face continual breakdowns in social structures.

Most of the scriptures are written about the interim times – between Eden and Heaven. They make it clear God is intimately concerned with our relationships. Not just our immediate families and friends. But with the structures of our society by which we relate to a great number of other human beings simultaneously.

This interest of God can be seen in the way families grow into nations.

- God is specially interested in one nation,
- God has a special agreement with Israel,
- Through Israel's ancestor, Abraham and his descendants, all the nations will bless themselves (Gen 12:1–3, *cf.* Is 49:5–7),
- This nation's destiny is therefore crucial in the history of the world,
- There emerges an increasingly complex pattern of relationships between nations, about which God is not neutral (See, for instance, Is 43:1–7).

The overarching narrative of scripture is about God's interest in what happens internationally as well as nationally and in every part of society.

The technical term for God's interest in all human beings – and the rest of creation – is God's providence.

This term summarises the Christian belief that God holds in existence people and nations, whether or not they acknowledge him or serve him.

- Paul tells the people in Athens who do not realise who is their creator (Acts 17:28) that "In him we live and move and have our being."
- The nations depend on God for their creation, preservation and redemption, and are like a drop in his bucket (Is 40:15; Acts 17:26–28).

Society in the Bible

No part of Scripture was written in the context of what today we would call a secular society.

- The different nations all had their own belief systems and their own gods.
- Nations usually had a dominant religion to which all its members adhered. This was the case of the people of God in Old Testament times. Their faith was in Yahweh, to which they believed they were committed by their ancestors,

and to which they were called anew in each generation (Deut 6:4–9).

- They were well aware that the nations around worshipped other gods, and that this shaped their social reality.

God ruled his people through a series of differing mechanisms:–

- patriarchs; Abraham, Isaac, Jacob,
- the great prophet; Moses,
- a series of Judges; Samson, Gideon,
- Kings; Saul, David, Solomon, etc.

The believers in Yahweh were also sometimes subject to the rule of other nations. For example:–

- to Assyria or Babylon in exile,
- to Persia in their return to the promised land,
- to an occupying force from Rome in the time of Jesus.

GOD AND GOVERNMENT

No single ideal pattern of social government is presented in scripture – though the writers are clear that some patterns are less than ideal.

Obviously the nation of Israel did not appreciate being governed from outside (Neh 1 & 2). But neither did its theologians believe the monarchy was the best form of government. For they believed it challenged the rule, which was God's alone. It was therefore reckoned to be an arrangement God permitted reluctantly (1 Sam 8).

When we think about social organisation today, it is therefore not a simple matter to offer Biblical reflection:–

- Only one nation is the chosen nation, though often promises which were made by God to Israel are 'claimed' by other nations.
- Few nations today are theocracies – intentionally trying to be governed by God alone.
- Very few nations today are populated by Christians alone – so experiments in organising society as if everyone were a converted Christian are unlikely to succeed.

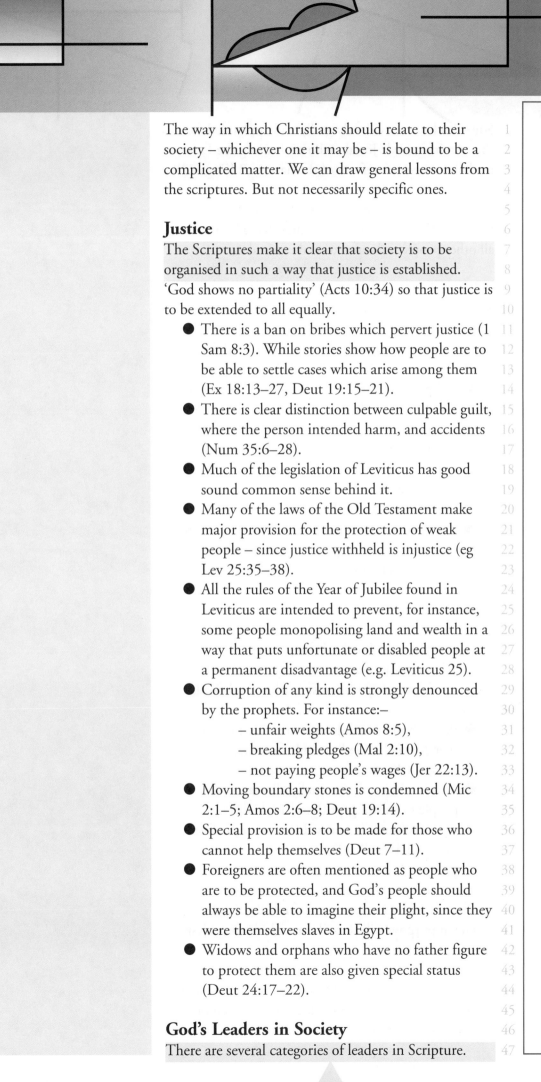

The way in which Christians should relate to their society – whichever one it may be – is bound to be a complicated matter. We can draw general lessons from the scriptures. But not necessarily specific ones.

Justice

The Scriptures make it clear that society is to be organised in such a way that justice is established. 'God shows no partiality' (Acts 10:34) so that justice is to be extended to all equally.

- There is a ban on bribes which pervert justice (1 Sam 8:3). While stories show how people are to be able to settle cases which arise among them (Ex 18:13–27, Deut 19:15–21).
- There is clear distinction between culpable guilt, where the person intended harm, and accidents (Num 35:6–28).
- Much of the legislation of Leviticus has good sound common sense behind it.
- Many of the laws of the Old Testament make major provision for the protection of weak people – since justice withheld is injustice (eg Lev 25:35–38).
- All the rules of the Year of Jubilee found in Leviticus are intended to prevent, for instance, some people monopolising land and wealth in a way that puts unfortunate or disabled people at a permanent disadvantage (e.g. Leviticus 25).
- Corruption of any kind is strongly denounced by the prophets. For instance:–
    - unfair weights (Amos 8:5),
    - breaking pledges (Mal 2:10),
    - not paying people's wages (Jer 22:13).
- Moving boundary stones is condemned (Mic 2:1–5; Amos 2:6–8; Deut 19:14).
- Special provision is to be made for those who cannot help themselves (Deut 7–11).
- Foreigners are often mentioned as people who are to be protected, and God's people should always be able to imagine their plight, since they were themselves slaves in Egypt.
- Widows and orphans who have no father figure to protect them are also given special status (Deut 24:17–22).

God's Leaders in Society

There are several categories of leaders in Scripture.

73

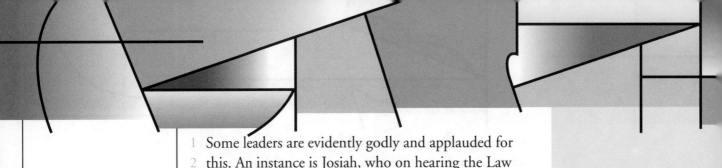

Some leaders are evidently godly and applauded for this. An instance is Josiah, who on hearing the Law read aloud began a reform of the nation (2 Kings 22).

In these cases we do not necessarily hear the full picture, although Scripture assumes that a leader, like all other people, is bound to make mistakes.

Other leaders are portrayed as being both very great and godly – yet as having made some major mistakes.

King David, for example, is reproved by God for:–
- His relationship with Bathsheba (2 Sam 11).
- His partiality for his son Absalom, which makes him have an unhealthy attitude to some of his faithful servants, after Absalom has rebelled and finally been killed (2 Sam 19).

On the other hand:–
- David listens to God (2 Sam 7).
- David establishes Jerusalem as the place where God is to be worshipped (2 Sam 6:16–23).
- David is merciful to his enemies (Saul in the cave, 1 Sam 24).
- David is commended for many other exploits.

Leaders outside God's Kingdom

The leaders of other nations may serve God's purposes, even if they recognise neither God nor his plans.
- Pharaoh promoted Joseph to prime minister, thereby saving God's people from famine (Gen 41:39–45).
- Another Pharaoh eventually allowed God's people to leave Egypt (Exod 13:17–21).
- Cyrus voluntarily released God's people from exile (Isa 45:1–7, 13).

All these stories make clear that leaders may collaborate with God, or oppose him. But God's sovereign purpose will prevail through them or despite them.

Old and New Testament alike encourage respect and collaboration where the ruler does not threaten prior loyalty to God himself.

The narratives of Joseph (Gen 41–50) and Daniel
(Dan 1–12) both make it clear that:–

- being a civil servant and serving a foreign ruler
  who does not confess Yahweh as God is not in
  itself wrong.
- compromise is always a possibility and there will
  be times when God's people need to make clear
  they are not primarily the servant of the ruler of
  the nation, but of the Ruler of the nations.
- despite turbulent fortunes, in which it is not
  always clear how the events will turn out, God is
  in control. His sovereign purpose will be fulfilled
  (Isaiah 46.8–11). "God sent me before you to
  preserve life" (Genesis 45.5).

Being 'at court' as a believer may mean God's people
can be helped in a very significant way.

- Nehemiah finds the opportunity he needs to
  petition the king to allow him to go to Jerusalem
  to rebuild the walls (Neh 1).
- Esther's story is another example of influence
  used for good to protect those whose interests
  were being destroyed.

Whatever kind of leader we may be faced with, we are
first commanded to love them as our neighbours, to
seek their good, and pray for them (1 Tim 2:1–4).

- We do not withhold from them what is their
  due, taxes (Rom 13:1–7).
- We do need to distinguish what is theirs and
  what is God's (Mark 12:13–17).

This rather subtle response of Jesus to the question
about paying taxes reminds us that we need to discern
what human rulers may justly require of us, and what
allegiance and obedience belongs to God alone.

Such decisions are immensely hard to make, and ones
which Christians in other centuries and parts of the
world have answered in different ways.

- Obedience is never to be unthinking – especially
  if it requires us to betray the gospel
  (Acts 5:27–32).
- We are to speak the truth to them, however hard
  that may be – especially if they hold our future
  in our hands (e.g. Acts 2:23).
- Sometimes speaking the truth may mean calling

them to repentance, as it did for John the Baptist, (Matt 3:7–12) or even denouncing them (Mark 6:17–29). But never in a way which means that we cease to pray for them.

THE PLACE OF WOMEN IN SOCIETY

There are passages in the Bible which describe women as equal partners with men.

Women are, for instance, equally in the image of God (Gen 1:27) capable of being leaders in society.

One of the Judges was a woman, Deborah, whose judgements were highly valued. This had established her among her contemporaries (Jdg 4:4) to such an extent that when danger threatened, Barak, the commander of the army, said to her: "If you will go with me, I will go; but if you will not go with me, I will not go" (Jdg 4:8).

There is a fine picture of a woman taking a lead in home and city in the book of Proverbs (Prov 31:10–31): "She opens her mouth with wisdom and the teaching of kindness is on her tongue". And a wonderful story of a woman's wisdom excelling that of her selfish and foolish husband (1 Sam 25).

There are also patterns of relationship described in Scripture which imply that women are owned and protected by men.

Though the story of Ruth implies this, it also makes it clear that women – collaborating within the framework of a God-given law about providing for widows – can outwit and out manoeuvre men.

This also highlights the importance of family and descendants in a pre-modern society, where security depended on younger people providing for older ones.

This is classically expressed in the 10 Commandments: "Honour your father and your mother" (Exod 20:12).

Some passages of Scripture appear really offensive about women.

- The preacher writes: "One (wise) man among a thousand I have found, but a (wise) woman among all these I have not found" (Ecc 7:28).
- Proverbs repeatedly warns about the dangers of women, who are snares and traps to men (e.g. Prov 5:3–6).

If this were all we found in Scripture, we might think the pattern of societies unashamedly sexist. Instead, it is simply clear the authors have a realistic view about the pervasiveness of human sinfulness which spoils relationships of every kind. And there are equally many examples of men being shown in a very poor light too. It is not only Jezebel who is condemned for her lust for power, but also her husband Ahab (1 Kings 21) and Rehoboam, for instance (1 Kings 12:1–19).

THE ENEMY

The Scriptures are frank about the complexity of life and the way people do not always remain in love and charity with their neighbours.

The Psalms, for instance, have a lot to say about 'the enemy' whether that is personal or national. "O God, do not keep silence … even now your enemies are in tumult, … they lay crafty plans against your people. … O my God, make them like whirling dust, like chaff before the wind" (Psa 83).

The language of the Psalms about enemies can be hard to understand. Being so used to hearing the command 'love your enemies', we find it impossible to admit there may be enemies. It is even harder to acknowledge that our feelings about them may be very strong.

The psalmist's prayers for God to overthrow enemies could be personal vindictiveness. But they could also be a recognition that God is Lord overall, and that one way he uses to establish right and justice in the world is the overthrow of the wicked.

It becomes clear that we cannot pray "thy kingdom come" about God's rule and his justice without realising that some people, or nations or leaders are set in flagrant opposition to God and God's ways.

77

1 We pray for God's rule to be established in places
2 where there is 'ethnic cleansing' or child prostitution,
3 or persecution of people for their beliefs, or some other
4 atrocities.
5
6 And we have to recognise that this prayer can be
7 answered in two ways.
8   ● By the repentance of the nation,
9   ● Or leaders concerned, leading to a change of
10   their policies.
11
12 Such changes do happen – as in South Africa. But in
13 other places no such repentance is forthcoming. There,
14 if God's rule is to be established, it may be only after
15 the overthrow of a wicked government.
16
17
SOCIETY AND WORK
19 Genesis Chapters 1–3 describe at least six aspects of
20 work which remain important today.
21
The Psychological Aspect of Work
23 Gen 1:27 describes how God created humans in his
24 own image – they were like him. They were made
25 great. And (verse 28) to work – mastering the world
26 and ruling over it. Humankind has been given a huge
27 job to match the greatness of its nature. The order is
28 important:–
29   ● First, men and women are given their worth.
30   ● Then, they are given their work.
31
32 Human worth comes before work. This challenges the
33 idea that people's worth depends on their work – that
34 to lose your job is to lose your value. Or that the more
35 important the job, the more important the person.
36
The Creative Aspect of Work
38 It is not the receiving of payment that turns an activity
39 into work, or doing something 'useful'. Gen 1:28
40 defines work in terms of mastering the created order.
41 This involves mastering the laws of nature, which is an
42 incredibly broad definition of work.
43
44 It means you can be at work mastering a
45 wordprocessor, or mastering the laws of a language, or
46 the laws of cooking, or the laws of accountancy, or the
47 laws of child-rearing.

The Sociological Aspect of Work

As a key part of their work, women and men are to build society:–

- They are to fill the earth (Gen 1:28).
- They are to do this in community. God saw that it was not good for the man to be alone (Gen 2:18).
- They are to rest (Gen 2:2,3).

Work should help to build community and to be done in community – which challenges us to improve relationships at work.

The Ecological Aspect of Work

Work should care for the environment. God planted a beautiful garden and commanded the man "to work it and take care of it" (Gen 2:15). The word 'subdue' in Gen 1:28 does not mean freedom to exploit creation. It has the idea of mastery, which can be very different. A loving master will want to bring out the best in his dog.

The Economic Aspect of Work

Work involves providing for human need. In the same breath that God tells the man to care for the garden, he says he is free to eat from any tree in it bar one (Gen 2:16–17). Part of caring for the world is to provide for human needs.

The Theological Aspect of Work

Work should create a home fit for God to live in. Gen 3:8 refers to God walking in the garden, with the implication that this was something that he did regularly. He had come into his creation to take a stroll.

GOD'S INTENTION FOR SOCIETY

At the heart of the gospel is *shalom*, a concept expressing God's desire to see all peoples and all things made whole and able to become all that God intends them to be.

- *Shalom* begins with a right relationship with God.
- *Shalom* involves right relationships with humans and even with the created order. These "right

Anthropological reflections on Missiological Issues, Paul Hiebert, Baker 1994, p210.

relationships are expressed in love and care for one another as people fully created in the image of God, no matter how broken or flawed."

- *Shalom* means to be more concerned for others than we are for ourselves and to commit ourselves to them no matter what their response may be.
- *Shalom* gives priority to building community and is particularly concerned for those who have in any way been marginalised or excluded from society in the past.

Isa 65:17–25 gives a wonderful image of the new *shalom* community, where:–

- Justice comes for the oppressed.
- Malnutrition and hunger is overcome.
- Each person lives in their own home and enjoys the fruit of their own labour.

Jesus is portrayed as the Prince of *Shalom*. In him all people and all things are made whole. They are brought into the unity and fellowship of that wonderful new *shalom* community, which will be fully manifest at the return of Christ.

As Christ's disciples, Christians are all called to participate with him in bringing glimpses of this shalom future of God into the world.

Alan Hawthorn, former Conservative politician, said: "If neighbours are strangers, truly there is no such thing as society".

Jesus reminds us to "Love your neighbour as yourself" (Luke 10:27). He goes on in the story of the good Samaritan to help us see that no-one is to be outside of our mercy and compassion.

As Henri Nouwen expresses it: "This is the vision that guides us. This vision makes us share one another's burdens, carry our crosses together and unite for a better world ... . The future has already begun and is revealed each time strangers are welcomed, the naked clothed, the sick and prisoners are visited, and oppression is overcome. Through these grateful actions the first glimpses of a new heaven and a new earth can be seen."

Compassion, A Reflection on the Christian Life, Henri Nouwen, Donald McNeill, Douglas Morrison, Image Books 1966, p134.

THE CHALLENGES WE FACE AS MEMBERS OF SOCIETY

LIVING FAITH SEVEN DAYS A WEEK

For most Christians, what drives their lives and determines their priorities is influenced by society at large rather than their Christian faith.

How much time and energy spent in their job, their sport and other activities is influenced by the way the world works rather than biblical values.

THE VALUES OF OUR SOCIETY	THE VALUES OF GOD'S KINGDOM
Tends to define a better future in terms of individuals getting ahead economically in their careers and personal lives.	Tends to define a better culture in terms of seeking God's righteousness, justice and shalom in the community.
Values materialism, consumerism and status. Holds on to life, rather than sharing it.	Values spirituality, servanthood, generosity to others and giving life away.
Inwardly focused on self-interest and improvement.	Outwardly focused – on the wellbeing of others and the group. In honour preferring one another.
Starts with us and ends with God. Jobs come first. A house in the suburbs comes first. Kid's activities come first. The Kingdom of God and its commitments come last.	Starts with the priorities of the Kingdom. Our sense of obedience to Christ first defines where our time and money go. Modern culture gets the leftovers.

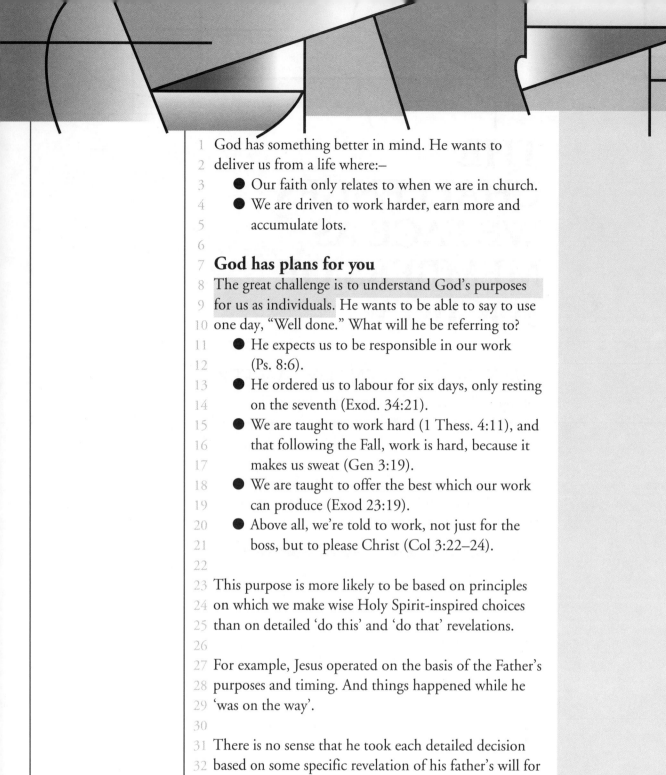

1 God has something better in mind. He wants to
2 deliver us from a life where:–
3   ● Our faith only relates to when we are in church.
4   ● We are driven to work harder, earn more and
5   accumulate lots.
6

God has plans for you

8 The great challenge is to understand God's purposes
9 for us as individuals. He wants to be able to say to use
10 one day, "Well done." What will he be referring to?
11   ● He expects us to be responsible in our work
12   (Ps. 8:6).
13   ● He ordered us to labour for six days, only resting
14   on the seventh (Exod. 34:21).
15   ● We are taught to work hard (1 Thess. 4:11), and
16   that following the Fall, work is hard, because it
17   makes us sweat (Gen 3:19).
18   ● We are taught to offer the best which our work
19   can produce (Exod 23:19).
20   ● Above all, we're told to work, not just for the
21   boss, but to please Christ (Col 3:22–24).
22

23 This purpose is more likely to be based on principles
24 on which we make wise Holy Spirit-inspired choices
25 than on detailed 'do this' and 'do that' revelations.
26

27 For example, Jesus operated on the basis of the Father's
28 purposes and timing. And things happened while he
29 'was on the way'.
30

31 There is no sense that he took each detailed decision
32 based on some specific revelation of his father's will for
33 that moment.
34

35 For example:–
36   ● Following Jesus and becoming His disciples
37   means giving up our lives so that we may truly
38   find them in Him. To become a disciple means
39   not only a change of heart but also a change of
40   life direction (Luke 9:57–10:4, 10:25–37,
41   14: 25–35; Matt 16:24–28;
42   Mark 10:29-31).
43   ● God's desire is to transform our lives completely
44   from upwardly mobile lives to outwardly
45   ministering lives (Rom 12:1–2, 9–21).
46   ● Suggests setting a goal in life is like an athlete
47   and setting aside everything that gets in the way

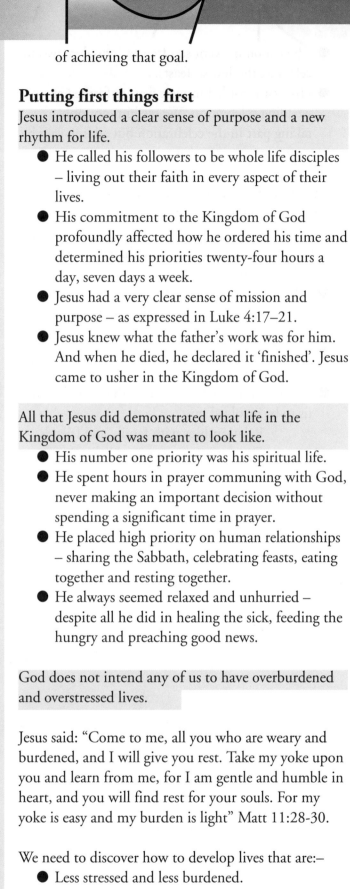

of achieving that goal.

Putting first things first

Jesus introduced a clear sense of purpose and a new rhythm for life.

- He called his followers to be whole life disciples – living out their faith in every aspect of their lives.
- His commitment to the Kingdom of God profoundly affected how he ordered his time and determined his priorities twenty-four hours a day, seven days a week.
- Jesus had a very clear sense of mission and purpose – as expressed in Luke 4:17–21.
- Jesus knew what the father's work was for him. And when he died, he declared it 'finished'. Jesus came to usher in the Kingdom of God.

All that Jesus did demonstrated what life in the Kingdom of God was meant to look like.

- His number one priority was his spiritual life.
- He spent hours in prayer communing with God, never making an important decision without spending a significant time in prayer.
- He placed high priority on human relationships – sharing the Sabbath, celebrating feasts, eating together and resting together.
- He always seemed relaxed and unhurried – despite all he did in healing the sick, feeding the hungry and preaching good news.

God does not intend any of us to have overburdened and overstressed lives.

Jesus said: "Come to me, all you who are weary and burdened, and I will give you rest. Take my yoke upon you and learn from me, for I am gentle and humble in heart, and you will find rest for your souls. For my yoke is easy and my burden is light" Matt 11:28-30.

We need to discover how to develop lives that are:–

- Less stressed and less burdened.
- Focused – like Christ's life – on the purposes of God.

Jesus' life too was one that involved much feasting and celebrating:–

The Co-operative Bank stopped dealing with corporate customers it considered were involved in 'unethical activities'. It promptly lost twelve customers – including two fox-hunting associations – but turned a £6 million loss into a £10 million pre-tax profit.

- The reason he went so often to Jerusalem was to celebrate the Jewish feasts.
- His first recorded miracle was performed at a wedding celebration. We see him not only taking part in the celebration but adding to it by turning water into wine.

Yet our faith today has become very serious business. The art of celebration has often been neglected.

Lives like this accomplish far more than those rooted in the values around us. Because:–

- All of our energy and time is then concentrated on God's purposes for our lives and not on our own.
- There is time for family and friends, as well as for Christian ministry.
- There is time for all the things that God intends us to be involved in:–
  - Relationships with family and friends,
  - Developing our spiritual lives,
  - Expressing our faith in practical ways.

DEVELOPING YOUR OWN PERSONAL MISSION STATEMENT

CREATING A MISSION STATEMENT

The more focused you are on what you are aiming at, the greater chance you have of hitting it.

One way to sharpen your aim is to create your own mission statement – individually or as a church or a family.

All the big corporations have one. So why not you?

A mission statement expresses what we see as the reason for our existence. It defines the focus of all we are and do. Not only of our vocation and work but for every area of our lives.

For Christians, this will reflect our understanding of God's purpose for our lives and for the human future – in the same way that it did for Jesus.

Your mission statement defines why you exist and the ways you intend to express this personally.

This is easier for some people to work out and express on paper than for others. So don't panic if you need help.

Jesus had his own clear mission statement – summed up in the words: "I have come that they may have life, and have it to the full." (John 10:10).

Everything Jesus did was focused on helping his disciples understand what that 'abundant life' looked like. That covered:–
- His work life.
- His personal time.
- His leisure time.

For that reason Jesus life focused on two major relationships:–
- With His Father – as shown through his focus on prayer and time with God.
- With humanity – as expressed through time

spent with his disciples in friendship and
ministry.

Where to begin

Take a sheet of paper – or sit down at your lap-top –
and prayerfully make some jottings. A useful approach
is to use a Word Pallette – see Page 100. Here you can
list words and ideas that you may want to include in
the finished picture.

As you make your list, do try to keep clear of vague
generalisations. 'To serve God' is not enough by itself.
How is this to be achieved. When and where?

Sense what God may be saying

Here are a few headings to run your mind round as
you add words and ideas to your pallette:–

- Think back over what you have heard or
  experienced during the past month about your
  relationship with God and his purposes.
- What do you sense God is nudging you towards
  in terms of your life's direction and priorities?
- What words or phrases from Scripture have
  struck you recently from a personal perspective?
- What has God been impressing on you in your
  times of quiet with him or in prayer with others?
- What areas of human need most make you want
  to respond?
- What experiences have you been through that
  God can use to make you more valuable to
  others?
- What gifts and abilities do you have that God
  may want to use in his service?
- What is it you are already doing that you sense
  God is pleased with?

If you need some extra inspiration, spend time
reflecting on Scripture. For example:–

- Isaiah 65:17–25; 58:5–9; 2:1–4; 35:1–7; 9:2–7.

Get the help and support you need

Although creating your own mission statement is a
personal thing, it should not stay that way.

Share the journey

- So you can create a more meaningful end result.
- So you can benefit from the help, support and

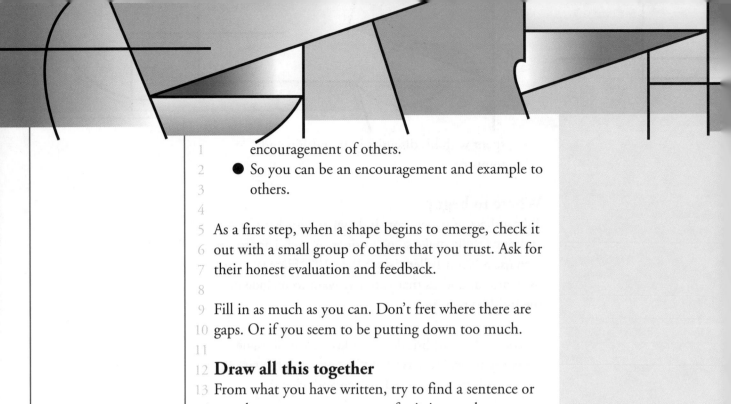

encouragement of others.
- So you can be an encouragement and example to others.

As a first step, when a shape begins to emerge, check it out with a small group of others that you trust. Ask for their honest evaluation and feedback.

Fill in as much as you can. Don't fret where there are gaps. Or if you seem to be putting down too much.

Draw all this together

From what you have written, try to find a sentence or two that sums up your sense of mission – what your life is to be all about. If possible, aim to include scripture.
- Make it simple and precise enough to memorise as you set out into the day.
- Make it inspirational – something that enthuses you.

Again, check what you have created with your small group. Use their input to help you fine tune it to fit who you are.

Don't expect to nail it down all at once. See it as 'work in progress' – and keep beavering away.

Simplify by including values and goals

Most likely your draft mission statement will be over crowded with tangents and aspirations and concerns. Ease the clutter in two ways.
1. Put your quality goals – things like 'integrity' and 'generosity' – under the Values heading.
2. Put measurable goals – like 'spend more time having fun' – under Goals. Goals are what you need to achieve in order to fulfil your mission.

Think about:–
- The lifetime achievements you may want to go for.
- The things you want to be different next week, month and year.
- The general actions and attitudes that touch your daily life.

As you make your list, remember, God's burden is

light and his yoke is easy. So don't create a heavy load
for yourself or others who are affected by your plans
and decisions.

Don't cover only seemingly Christian activities.
Include goals for every part of your life that flow
directly from your mission statement.

1
2
3
4
5
6
7
8
9
10
11
12
13
14
15
16
17
18
19
20
21
22
23
24
25
26
27
28
29
30
31
32
33
34
35
36
37
38
39
40
41
42
43
44
45
46
47

CELEBRATING THE KINGDOM OF GOD

CREATIVE
TIMESTYLE AND LIFESTYLE
RESPONSES

Becoming a voice for those who have no voice

Christine Sine grew up in Australia and trained as a medical doctor. Her plan was to spend her life working in general practice in that country.

But as a young Christian she was challenged by Is 58: 6-9. Through this passage of Scripture God motivated her to spend a couple of years as a missionary doctor. In the early '80s Christine spent several weeks working in the refugee camps in Thailand, something that totally changed the direction of her whole life. The impact of having children die in her arms drove her back to the Bible. The next step was to study what Christian responsibility to the poor really means.

Then came a decision to be involved in missions for the rest of her life – the next ten years were spent developing the medical work on the YWAM mercy ship the Anastasis among the poor of Africa, Asia and Central America.

From a distance
At the beginning of the '90s Christine moved to the United States and faced the question 'How am I to live out my concern for the poor in this new environment?'

The words of Prov 31: 8,9 - to be a voice for the voiceless –

The impact of having children die in her arms drove Christine back to the Bible.

seemed to sum up her desire to be an advocate for those who had no voice in society. It has become the focus of her sense of missionary call today. Christine now works with her husband, Tom, to awaken churches and individual Christians to the needs of those marginalised within society - helping them find creative ways to respond to needs.

Sometimes even times of social celebration revolve around this theme. One year, Christine and Tom arranged an Africa night.

○ People came in African dress or brought something that reminded them of Africa.
○ Christine showed her slides from Africa.
○ Food included an African meal of Ugandan groundnut stew, Ethiopian salad and couscous.
○ The evening ended with prayer for Rwanda and other needy parts of Africa.

It's OK to be young

John wants to use his gifts to mentor and encourage potential young leaders.

John is a young adult from Alabama. His heart is particularly stirred by the lives of young people who go off the rails, either through involvement in drugs or violence or suicide. He sees these tragedies as the loss of potential leaders for the Body of Christ and wants to use his gifts to mentor and encourage potential young leaders to become all God

intends them to be.
John feels his mission statement revolves around 1 Tim 4:12: "Don't let anyone look down on you because you are young, but set an example for the believers in speech, in life, in love, in faith and in purity."

John has re-ordered his personal life and priorities to put God's purposes first in all areas.

Co-op living in Hackney

Rent or a mortgage present young people with particularly heavy burdens. The demands are such that the time needed to earn the money is at the expense of having a balanced and God-centered lifestyle.

Members of the United Reform Church in Hackney are facing the issue by working to reduce

Church members are reducing their costs by living co-operatively.

their costs by living co-operatively rather than individualistically.

○ Many church members live

in the same street and so share cars, washing machines and other household appliances.
○ Some are exploring buying houses together.
○ The church runs a food co-operative for low income families and is setting up a credit action scheme to provide credit to those without access to it.

Co-op mortgage in Vancouver

A group of Mennonites in Vancouver, British Columbia, found by working co-operatively they could greatly reduce their mortgage burden. On top of their regular mortgage payments they all paid into a co-operative bank account and then began paying out mortgages based on

those who had greatest need.

Debt free in seven years.

These people continued to pay into the fund and much to everyone's surprise, all of them were debt free in seven years rather than 30.

Banquet of faith

The Christians of Host Community in Hackney embrace a richly multicultural community and are exploring ways to celebrate these differences.

They recently hosted a mini arts festival at the church, ending with a banquet and serving a rich variety of food from the diverse nationalities in the area.

Innovative worship

An Anglican vicar has developed innovative liturgical worship that relates to young people.

He has established a monthly pattern:-

○ one meditative Taize-based service with a simple bible meditation.

○ two Eucharistic and teaching based services following an traditional Anglican liturgy.
○ one service using more creative arts and focused on the Christian festival of the season from the liturgical calendar, thus living out the whole gospel story through the year in their worship.

What is really important

A young southeast couple recently had a wake-up call. They realized that the long hours Steve was working – and the pressures his job demanded – placed severe restrictions on their lives. They no longer had time for prayer, Christian service or active church involvement.

Steve no longer had time for prayer, or Christian service, so he left his job.

They are now in the process of a major re-evaluation of their lives.

○ They have decided to sell their house to reduce their mortgage burden.
○ Steve is looking for a new job where he works fewer hours.

As a result, they will both be available for the important work of the church and the human needs in their town.

Parenting skills for the poor

Susan has always been well off and lives in a beautiful part of London. However she was concerned for the young women she met from the nearby housing estate who did not have the first clue about how to bring up their children.

She began holding parenting classes on the estate. And soon discovered the young and inexperienced women - many

The young women from the nearby housing estate did not have the first clue about how to bring up their children.

from broken homes and often bringing up children alone - were keen to learn.

Some started asking questions about the Christian faith and eventually made a commitment

to Christ. Tentatively, they then asked Susan if they would now be welcome at her church, which they still perceived as a place only for those who were well off and who already had a life together.

Cross connections for the kingdom

Trevor and Dorothy Davies are a British couple whose whole lives reflect their concern for justice. They are particularly concerned for the plight of women and girl children around the world.

The Davieses have lived in Geneva for 25 years, actively involved in fighting the cause for development and human rights issues at UN commissions and world conferences. They promote awareness.

Cross-Connections International was formed by the pair to use their expertise to build bridges between Christian organisations and the United Nations.

Trevor and Dorothy's desire is:-
O To promote development and human rights issues.
O To raise awareness over religious liberty by networking, building coalitions and sharing resources.

Visual Imagery in Lincoln

Creative and innovative forms of worship and new church plants geared towards youth have sprung up across the UK in the past few years.

One example is Sense - an alternative worship service for the 18+, mainly students, based at New Life Christian Centre in Lincoln.

It uses:-
O a very flexible format with a variety of music styles in as many creative combinations as possible.

O visual imagery incorporating video, computer graphics and slides.
O projected images to help interpret what is said, done

or sung.
Each service is different as the creativity team fosters creativity through the use of dance, self expression, art and drama.

Environmental law in North Africa

Our own individual lives and choices can have a significant impact on others. Paul, a young lawyer from New Zealand, could not find a job when he first graduated from law school so he decided to work in Fiji for a couple of years.

Paul was asked to investigate the legal aspects of the environmental impact of international trade agreements.

As a result, he became deeply interested in environmental law and returned to New Zealand for post-graduate studies in this subject.

Now, with his family, he plans to work in this vital area of advocacy, helping governments in North Africa understand the environmental implications of the international trade agreements they make.

From the piano to the poor

Cynthia's got a sense of purpose from her mission statement: "To go where most needed, and do what is most necessary."

As a youngster, she wanted to become a concert pianist. But as she looked at the needy world and heard about the poor and the sick in India and Nepal, Cynthia realized that God was calling her to become a doctor and work in these needy parts of the world.

Not long after, Cynthia and her husband went to Nepal. They

Cynthia does what is most necessary by encouraging young Christians to commit their lives more fully to God and consider a missionary calling

were blessed with three children and she recognized that to 'do what is most necessary' at that point in her life more reflected her need to concentrate on bringing up her family.

As the children grew and became more independant, Cynthia was able to spend more of her time practicing medicine again.

Today, Cynthia and her husband live in the United States.

They are doing what is most necessary by encouraging young Christians to commit their lives more fully to God and consider a missionary calling.

Oneof the ways Cynthia is able to do this is through the ministry of music – as a concert pianist.

Transforming a school

One London church took note that research shows the provision of stable adult role models outside the family often provides

Stable adult role models work wonders with youngsters at risk.

stability and support for children at risk.

They mobilized a committed handful of volunteers to go into the local inner city primary school. There they read regularly to the children and often formed

'big brother' 'big sister' relationships.

It worked wonders in the lives of

the children and the teachers feel less stressed and are grateful for the relationships and prayer support of the volunteers.

Foster grandparents

A large number of retired people, many of whom have moved away from their families, have relocated in Tauranga, one of the warmest parts of New Zealand. Barry, who attends the local Baptist church, introduced one of them there.

Barry noticed many of the young families in the church

were young single parents with few if any male role models for their children.

Missing his grandchildren, Barry organized some friends into an 'adopt a grandchild' programme, which matched retired people with young children desperately in need of some parenting.

Single finds her place

Ruth, a single British woman in her 50s, lives in a small flat on her own in Texas. But close friends nearby have adopted her as one of the family.

They have given Ruth the

privilege of being godmother to two of their three boys, a responsibility she takes very seriously. She takes them to sports events on the weekends, has them over for meals and is always included in family

celebrations such as birthdays and Christmas.

One of the family.

Ruth has found her place in God's church family.

Shalom in Easterhouse

Community development provides a hand up rather than a handout. This gives people the power to participate in solving their own

- ○ Poor healthcare and diet.
- ○ Lack of economic opportunity.
- ○ Stress in this tough, crime-ridden environment.

were often charged interest rates as high as 100 per cent a week.

Working with The Sisters of Charity:-
- ○ They helped local people form the North Easterhouse Credit Union, which now has 500 members.
- ○ They helped set up a food co-operative.
- ○ They used FARE's minibus to bring food back at affordable prices from the nearest large supermarket.

Interest rates are as high as 100 per cent a week.

problems, rather than being permanently dependent on others for their survival.

In Easterhouse, on the fringes of Glasgow, women die five years younger than in Glasgow itself. The reasons are:-

Concerned about the injustices he saw, Bob Holman joined with other residents to form FARE (Family Action in Rogerfield and Easterhouse). They saw the great problem - people had no ready source for financial loans and

This is a tangible expression of the shalom love of God.

Single mum finding a focus in Haiti

Sometimes it can be the children who provide the challenge for the family. Leila, a single parent, has always worried about the loneliness and isolation she expected after her children left home.

Then her 13-year-old son went on a short-term mission trip to Mexico. And everything changed for him and for the whole of his family. He drastically changed his spending habits and attitude to lose his material possessions. He began saving all his pocket money so he could repeat the trip the following year. This was so radical that Leila and her daughter decided to give the trip a go too.

Two years later Leila joined four other families in a mission trip to Haiti. For three weeks she and her two teenagers lived in a village with no running water and no electricity. They dug

ditches, fed children and told Bible stories.

Now Leila's whole life focus has changed. She is no longer afraid

of what she will do when her children leave home in a few years time. She intends to commit the rest of her life to helping others.

Reconciliation walks in Turkey and Auschwitz

In response to the atrocities of the Crusades, the Reconciliation Walk organized by Lynn Green and others has passed through Europe and into the Middle East seeking out Muslim, Jewish and governmental leaders to ask forgiveness.

This is a wonderful example of how reconciliation can have a huge impact in healing wounds that may have festered for centuries.

In Germany, Hans, a Lutheran pastor, takes groups of German Christians to Auschwitz each year and spends several days taking them around the former concentration camp and viewing the horrors of the Holocaust.

Only at the end of the trip does Hans make space for them to pray prayers of repentance for the sins of their country against the Jews and for reconciliation between Christians and Jews.

Outbidding Coca Cola in Belize

The Christian Environmental Association is a US-based organization that is helping to motivate young adults to defend the environment. Its six campuses around the world provide courses in environmental management and sustainable development.

One of their centres is in Belize, Central America. It is situated right in the middle of the rainforest and is designed to have as little environmental impact as possible:-

O The buildings are modelled after Mayan structures, with thatched roofs and wooden floors.
O Electric power is provided by photovoltaic energy cells.
O Raised pathways between the buildings provide uninterrupted access for small animals.

While purchasing the property, CEA discovered Coca Cola wanted to buy 8,000 acres of prime rainforest to provide orange juice for the American market.

This put the natural fauna at risk as the remaining forests would be too small to cope with the migration that would take place. The young leaders got into a bidding war with Coca Cola – and won. The land, now established as the Eden Conservancy, will preserve the rainforest into the future and will provide a corridor for the animals to travel between national parks.

Jubilee Trust for Millennium III

One creative response to concerns for justice is the Jubilee 2000 Coalition. This has tied together concern about Third World debt and the Biblical concept of Jubilee. The aim is to give a debt-free start to a billion people. The mission is to lift the major burden of poverty internationally.

Jubilee 2000 is equated with the abolition of slavery in the 18th century and describes its

The aim is to give a debt-free start to the millennium for a billion people.

supporters as "the new abolitionists". Their objective is to promote the campaign for debt cancellation through "harnessing the interest and goodwill of millions of people who will create an unstoppable force for change".

They are seeking to enlist the aid of Christians worldwide to see the debt of at least one African country abolished by the year 2000.

Mission trip to Latin America

Larry, an ophthalmologist from Canada, took part in short-term mission trips to Mexico and the Dominican Republic several years in a row.

Life transforming.

Larry's children were teenagers and they not only attended the trips but became part of the team, screening patients for operations, taking blood pressure and assisting with post-operative care. It was a life transforming experience for all of them. And two of Larry's children are now in mission service.

Care for Creation

Rocha Trust, a UK-based Christian conservation group, provides resource packs for local churches and individuals wanting to get involved in creation care.

The pack offers:-

O Biblical teaching on stewardship,
O Information to show how the foods we eat and our farming and lifestyle practices impact the environment.

MISSION STATEMENT DRAFTS

Draft 1

MISSION STATEMENT

The reason I/we exist is …

To: _____

_____

_____

_____

_____

_____

_____

_____

Draft 2

MISSION STATEMENT

The reason I/we exist is …

To: _____

_____

_____

_____

_____

Values

I/we will hold fast to …

_____

_____

_____

_____

Goals

I/we will set out to achieve …

_____

_____

_____

_____

Draft 3

MISSION STATEMENT

The reason I/we exist is ...

To: _____

_____

_____

_____

_____

Values

I/we will hold fast to ...

_____

_____

_____

_____

_____

_____

_____

Goals

I/we will set out to achieve ...

_____

_____

_____

_____

_____

_____

_____

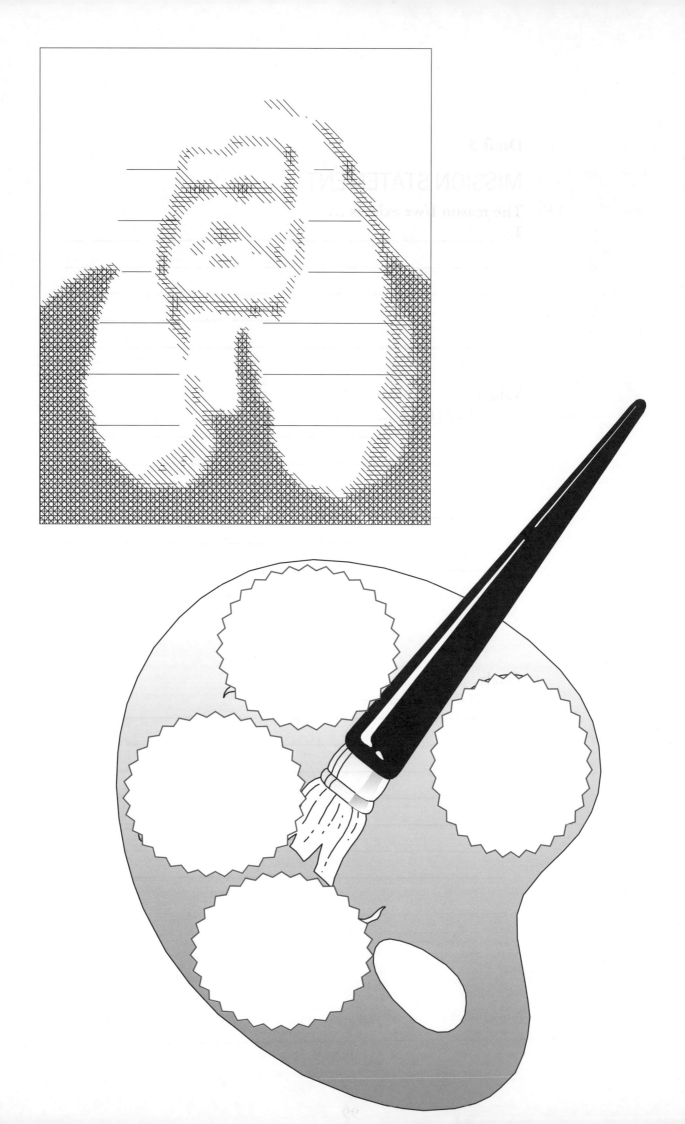

TIMETABLES

	7.00	8.00	9.00	10.00	11.00	12.00	13.00	14.00	15.00	16.00	17.00	18.00	19.00	20.00	21.00	22.00	23.00	24.00
Mon																		
Tue																		
Wed																		
Th																		
Fri																		
Sat																		
Sun																		

	7.00	8.00	9.00	10.00	11.00	12.00	13.00	14.00	15.00	16.00	17.00	18.00	19.00	20.00	21.00	22.00	23.00	24.00
Mon																		
Tue																		
Wed																		
Th																		
Fri																		
Sat																		
Sun																		

1
2
3
4
5
6
7
8
9
10
11
12
13
14
15
16
17
18
19
20
21
22
23
24
25
26
27
28
29
30
31
32
33
34
35
36
37
38
39
40
41
42
43
44
45
46
47